It is I, Amadeus

Channeled Messages from Spirit

Frances Pullin

It is I, Amadeus

Copyright © 2014 by Frances Pullin

All rights reserved. No part of this book may be reproduced, in whole or in part, by any mechanical, photographic, or electronic process. It may not be stored in a retrieval system, transmitted or otherwise copies for public or private use without prior permission of the publisher.

Editor: Jean-Noel Bassior
Interior Design: Jera Publishing
Cover Design: Laura Gordon

First Edition

ISBN: 978-0-9903932-0-7

Dedication

This book, *It is I, Amadeus. Channeled Messages From Spirit* is dedicated to Damon Andrew Clemens Pullin. Born April 11, 1970. Crossed into the Light, October 26, 2003.

It is his essence that we remember with love and laughter. He was a kindred soul and quick-witted. He is missed by all who knew him and we await our turn to join him on the Other Side.

Introduction

It seems like a lifetime ago, and it was. Holding my sister's hand to give her courage as she first dipped her toe in the pool of the psychic realm; being there the first time she realized that there were Powers to Be that saw who you really were, that understood and could guide you. Powers with enormous understanding of what she did not comprehend; helping to see beyond what was in front of her.

My sister, Frances, took that first step and continued to carefully nudge slowly into the psychic world, curious but cautious. Over the years, there were times when she took me with her to psychic readings, but while she was open to being "read," I was more difficult. It was her openness to the metaphysical world that helped these spiritual readers give her insight and knowledge that fueled her interest – and this left her wanting even more.

Then came the day that my sister's world crashed, when she lost her special boy in death. The worst thing that could happen had. Over the next few years, in her quest to understand what had happened and why, she discovered spiritual teachings that eased her pain and helped her let go of her beloved Damon. She was always excited to share these insights with me, even though there were times when, though interested, I really didn't understand everything she was saying.

Frances will never stop missing Damon, but the metaphysical world has helped give her the peace that comes from knowing he is happy; knowing he's aware of his sweet daughter Morgan's life and accomplishments; knowing we will all meet up with him one day to share these memories once again.

My sister's journey has reinforced what I always knew – how strong, loving and beautiful her soul is. Sharing her story allows others to see that as well, as they find love of self through her guidance.

Contents

Part One 1

1. A Source-Sent Message 3
2. An Unusual Dinner Party 7
3. Who Was Damon? 11
4. Fate Brings Kevin to Me 19
5. A Vacation Like No Other 27
6. My Spiritual Journey Begins 31
7. Psychics Become a Part of My Life 37
8. Meditation My Way 41
9. The Last Piece of My Puzzle 49
10. Learning Through Living Life 55
11. Synchronicity Visits Us All **59**
12. Stepping onto My True Path 63
13. Knowing Source 69

Part Two 73

14. The Journey Continues 75
15. It is I, Amadeus 79
16. The Others 83
17. Sharing Private Notes 89
18. Healing 97

19	Learning Trust	101
20	Following the Path	107
21	Meditation Choices	111
22	A Day in the Life of a Channel: Me	119
23	Truth in Truth	123
24	A New Year, 2009	137
25	Ancestors Revealed	145
26	Moving Further Through Grief	149
27	Learning to Communicate with Others in Spirit	155

Acknowledgements ... 161
Endorsements ... 165

Part One

Chapter One
A Source-Sent Message

It is I, Amadeus. Greetings, Sweet One. Greetings to your audience! I am here with you today to bring a message of love to all who enter here! Your mother, who resides on the Other Side, has asked me to bring in a greeting from myself as your story begins. After all, it is all about your journey, beginning with the passing of your son and continuing with the lessons that I and Others teach you. My message to the world is of love and peace. It all begins with love of self. When you have conquered love of self, the love you emanate knows no bounds. Go now and tell the story as you know it!

With love, Amadeus.

The stillness of the night was shattered by the shrill ring of the telephone down the hall. Is that why I never kept a phone in my bedroom? Did I know that someday I'd receive that 1:00 a.m. call? My son, Kevin II, handed me the phone. The frantic voice of my other son's girlfriend, Sarah, was on the other end. Damon was not breathing. Yes, the paramedics were there; yes I could speak with them. They asked us to come. No, not to the hospital. To his apartment in Studio City.

They would not tell me anything more. Were they sure, I kept asking, that they wanted us to come to his apartment? Did they realize we lived in Orange County – an hour away? My husband, visibly shaken by my insistent questions, took the phone and listened, but did not speak. Finally, he said stoically, "OK." Then he turned to me: "Let's go."

It was then that I knew my oldest son was gone.

I became numb and could not think of what to do next. I headed toward the bathroom, followed by Kevin II, who watched in amazement as I pulled toothpaste and toothbrush from the cabinet and began brushing my teeth. Who knows why I did this? Was it to kiss my son his last goodbye with sweet breath? Was it to suspend time for just a moment, to enter a safe space where I didn't have to think about what was really happening? I guess you never really know what you'll do in sudden shock and pain, but as I glanced at Kevin II, I saw that he got it. He knew. I asked if he wished to come with us, but he stood fast and grimly refused.

My husband, Kevin, and I set out for the hour-long journey to Studio City, and I continued to babble about why they did not want us to come to the hospital. I wanted the truth, but Kevin, now in survival mode, did not want to say out loud what he knew. In the midst of the dark of night, we made a wrong turn, and I had to call the house for directions. The paramedics were still there. They gave me directions, but still did not break the news to Damon's numb mother. Never having liked cell phones, I rarely carried one, but this night it was a blessing to have one in my hands. It was my connection to those who hovered over my son's body.

When we arrived at the apartment, Damon was covered with a sheet. I took his hand and held it, crying quietly. I had little emotion. Grief had arrived like a shawl and covered me with a sadness I never knew existed. I was speechless and in shock. Damon had had a massive heart attack and died immediately. It was to be the last time I kissed him. His body was so lifeless, but still warm. Was this nothing more than a harsh nightmare? No, he had left this world at age 33. I never dreamed I would tell him goodbye so soon.

The grief paralyzed me, and I was not sure what to do next. I moved toward his girlfriend, Sarah, and held her in my arms as tears flowed down her face. I always think I have to be the strong one with the children and not cry, so here I was, in the worst grief of my life, tending to another whose pain was breaking her heart. It was she who had found Damon unresponsive, called the paramedics, and let them in. It was she who had to describe their last evening together – what they ate and drank, what the evening was like before he got out of bed to lie on the sofa to ease his intense indigestion. Oh, it was this tender woman who'd been the last person to say "I love you" before his life ended. I held her in my arms and helped her to the bedroom. She then called her best friend to drive over and take her home with her for the long night ahead.

There was a knock on the door, and the coroner arrived. My husband brought Sarah and me to the living room, where I was able to say a last goodbye to my son; then he asked us to return to the bedroom. Kevin did not leave Damon, but stayed to supervise and make sure his body was treated with kindness. Later, he told me how they'd wrapped him in a body bag and carried him down the stairs. There would be an autopsy, as he had not been under a doctor's care. The autopsy ultimately ruled out drugs of any kind, and the death certificate simply stated: Atherosclerotic Heart Disease. In layman's terms, it meant heart attack.

In the ensuing months, I learned that grief is a selfish emotion, because it was all about me. Damon was gone, and I could not celebrate his "return to the Universe to sit with Source." I knew he was "home," but I wanted him back. I wanted him strong and healthy and filled with the vitality that the young possess as they continue their journey into what still lies ahead of them. For Damon, there was no continuing journey on Earth. Why was he chosen to leave at the tender age of 33, when so many cruel and inhumane souls still walk the earth? I have shed many a tear. It has gotten easier to be happy for him, but the story is a long one. The date was October 26, 2003. Never to be remembered in full, never to be forgotten.

And so it is that I began my spiritual journey that led to this book. It is without much fanfare that this, my tale, unfolds...

Chapter Two

An Unusual Dinner Party

It is I, Amadeus. Many years ago, we sought your attention. You were frightened, yet curious. This dinner party set your mind in motion, and you feel it uncanny that after all of these years, you are now a channel. Once frightened, now in reverence.

Love and Light, Amadeus.

It was thirty-five years ago that I was first introduced to the psychic world at my parents' dinner table. They had invited me and my then husband, Steve, to dinner. My sister and a family friend, Frank Dixon, had also been invited. Frank, on his way to Texas from California for a vacation, had stopped in Tucson to visit with my parents for the day. Dinner was filled with chatter as Steve and I got to know Frank. I was curious about him, since my parents rarely had company, and I wanted to know why he had been chosen to join us.

My parents had met Frank while they were living in Elk Grove, a small community near Sacramento, California. He had been to dinner at their home, and my sister had met him then. She was still living at home at the time and attending the local high school. My mom and dad had since moved back to Tucson (along with my sister, brother and, of course, the cat), and they were eager to enjoy their friend Frank in their new surroundings.

'When dinner was over, the conversation turned to religion, and then to the spirit world. I had never met anyone like Frank, who had such immense knowledge of God, Jesus, and religious teachings. I was fascinated and settled in for a long, lovely evening, as I wanted more of this religious energy. He seemed so confident about his knowledge of God and religion, and that intrigued me.

Conflicting feelings battled within me when Frank suggested a séance, but he seemed so clear in his religious knowledge that I felt comfortable enough to agree. Still, I will never forget my deep-seated fear, as we moved forward, that Source – my name for God or a Higher Power – would not like the direction the evening was taking. Growing up, I'd been taught in church that the spirit world was the work of the devil – and yet here I was in the comfort of my parents' home, and they seemed happy enough to move forward. How could I resist, given that I was their child, and (at that time in my life) did as they wished?

I have since learned that the spirit world is *not* the work of the devil, but quite the opposite. In fact, I now know that this realm is based on unconditional love. (Frank used the word "God," but in my attempt to bring this book to those who do not believe in God, or who call this higher power by a different name, I use the term "Source." Today, when my Guides and Others speak through me, they use "God," so later on, when I share their messages with you, I use that term to preserve their exact wording.)

Frank asked for everyone's agreement before he began. I paused briefly and then, after deep contemplation, nodded yes. I reasoned that my fear was based on those church teachings I'd grown up with, but Frank's intelligence, quiet presence, and his caring and affection for my mom and dad put me at ease.

Frank said that each of us could ask a question when his Spirit Guide came through. He explained that she was a woman named Shay, and when he spoke, a woman's voice *did* come through him! At that moment, I knew it was no longer him, but Spirit speaking. When it was my turn to ask a question, I told Shay about a dream that I'd relived over and over. As I spoke, Shay told my sister to take my hand because I seemed frightened. This surprised me, as my sister is eight years younger than me and was in high school at the time – and I was the mother of two!

Shay went on to explain that the dream was in my subconscious, and that it came from a past life. It seems I was married to a German officer in World War II, and since I was living in a city, not a rural village, the war was an everyday, real-life nightmare! During the battles, I found myself running from one building to the next, trying to outrun the shells that pummeled the city. I always felt such fear when this dream came to me, and would awaken feeling that it was so real. But Shay's explanation that it was a past-life memory felt so right, and to this day, that dream has never returned, no matter how many times I repeat this story.

Shay then spoke to my husband, Steve, telling him that he had so much love surrounding him, but took none of it in and gave none of it out. Knowing this to be true, I began to think that there might be something of value to this eerie evening, after all. Then Shay had another message for me. She knew I was giving a friend some valuable help, although my husband said I was just being used and to drop her. To my amazement, Shay recommended that I continue the friendship. Interestingly enough, that friend is still part of my life, and Steve is no longer my husband.

All the guests, including my parents, received messages pertinent to them, but those messages are not part of my memory. I do recall, though, that the evening ended with lightheartedness and pleasure, leaving me a believer in all that had happened and determined to delve into what I had learned.

Chapter Three

Who Was Damon?

It is I, Amadeus. Greetings, Sweet One! You wish to let your audience know who this Spirit, Damon, was during this lifetime. This section will reveal what a wonderful Spirit he was and why he was so revered in this lifetime.

Love, Amadeus.

> Damon Andrew Clemens Pullin. Born April 11, 1970
> Crossed into the Light October 26, 2003

Damon was the second of my children. He was born in Tucson, Arizona, in the middle of a beautiful spring day. As I lay there in the delivery room, my doctor strolled in. He was in his tennis clothes. He grinned widely and asked, "Why have you pulled me from my game?"

"You told me today was the day, and so it is," I teased back in return. Then the pain gripped my body and another contraction brought Damon crowning, and soon thereafter into the world.

Can you imagine a mother not wanting visitors because her baby boy was so unattractive? Oh yes, I was a proud mama, but his sister, who'd been ten days late, was completely filled out and robust. In contrast,

Damon was a skinny little thing, and in my world, surrounded by young and impressionable, non-spiritual friends, I could only think about the robust baby I wanted to show off. The only choice, of course, was to take him home with love and abandon. The doctor wanted to keep us in the hospital, as Damon had a slight case of jaundice, but money was tight and we had no insurance. Finally, they agreed to let us take him home to our townhouse with my promise that we would return each day for a check-up until he was fully recovered.

I took him out into the sunshine several times a day for short periods to give him what he needed to heal, and in three days, the doctor wished us well and released him. His father did not believe in wasting money on insurance, so we had no family policy. I had a policy on myself, but back in 1970, an insurance company would not cover the cost of a baby born to a mother whose husband was not on the policy too. Of course, we found out that little piece of information in the small print, after submitting the bills from the first doctor's visit. (Always read the small print!) So, due to the stubborn man I had married, we found we had put our child in jeopardy and ourselves in debt. Those were the days, my friends. But this was part of the journey.

It took no time at all for this lean little guy to gulp down his food and fill out to the point of untold adorable. Pure and loving, my little boy was at home. I decided that, with the cost of daycare, a work wardrobe, and gas for the car, it was better for me to stay at home and do daycare on my own. I put out the word that I was willing to care for other children in my home, and soon I'd created a thriving daycare business. I have always felt that I wanted to raise my children myself and not entrust them to strangers. If I wanted my values instilled in them, they were going to have to hear my teaching, day in and day out.

The following year, we purchased a small, three-bedroom home on a cul-de-sac alongside our good friends. We all had little boys, and two of us had a girl, too. Damon and his older sister, Michelle, grew up in a loving environment and became good friends, not just siblings. On a hot summer day, you could find them running through the sprinklers, jubilant, without a care in the world. We loved our little yellow house and were proud homeowners.

Twelve houses and over a dozen fun-loving kids on this peaceful cul-de-sac meant birthday parties, swimming in plastic pools, and little children constantly racing their Big Wheels up and down the street. (A Big Wheel has one very large wheel in front and two smaller wheels behind. It's low to the ground and moves as fast as little legs can pump.) Damon was the daredevil! He would race as fast as he could and then turn the wheel and blast back down the sidewalk. His face was always friendly and smiling, with more mischief than the rest of the pack.

It was Damon who found the ladder leaning up against the house where his father had left it and neglected to sense the danger it might cause. Up he went – pure mischief and exploration! He went all the way to the top, where he toppled back down to the ground. I found out about it when Michelle came into the house crying, telling me Damon was hurt. In my fear, I raced from the kitchen, lifted him from the ground, saw he was not injured, and spanked his behind. It was the only response I could summon, driven by my fear of his reckless behavior and that he would get hurt again. I continued to react to his antics that way. I was always fearful for his safety. His sister did not cause me that angst, as she was quieter than Damon, dainty, and not at all mischievous. Perhaps there had always been a knowing he was not going to be with me in his physical body all of my life.

The Damon stories continued as he and Michelle grew older. He was bold, daring, and always looking for the next real-life adventure. In contrast, Michelle was a quiet little girl, her head often buried in a book of fantasy, racing off to distant places in her mind.

But as the children grew, their parents grew apart. Not knowing how to fix the hole in our hearts, Steve and I found a new home to move into, trying to recapture the happiness of earlier years. We sold the little yellow house of so many memories and ventured onward and upward to a tri-level that had three bedrooms upstairs. The living room, dining room and kitchen were on the main floor, and one bedroom was downstairs with its own bathroom.

We tried to love this new house, and we tried to fall back in love, but it was not to be; after three months, Steve walked out and left me in anguish and tears, crumpled on the kitchen floor. It was then that Damon and Michelle's beautiful, strong sibling bond seemed to embrace them, and they clung to each other through the pain of seeing their parents separate and divorce. Not understanding all that was going on with mommy and daddy; they talked to each other, so as not to ask me questions they knew might make me cry. It was a trying time.

By that time I was selling real estate, but knew it was time to get another job where I could be home at night and know the bills would be covered without question. I've never been much of a risk-taker, so I applied for, and accepted, a job with a savings and thrift association as a secretary. Those high school premonitions of having to support myself had, in fact, become true. The subsequent divorce brought $200 a month in child support that was almost never paid. I had to learn that it was a bonus if it came at all. Life was becoming difficult, as I was a young mother, 25 years old, with two small children and the daunting task of feeding and clothing them alone. Hello Goodwill and Kmart! Goodbye department stores.

Steve's mother proved to be a generous grandma, even after the divorce. Each year before school started, she would take us shopping, and Damon and Michelle would each get six pair of jeans and twelve undies, socks and tee shirts. She'd also buy two pairs of shoes, jackets, and all of their school supplies, including the metal lunch box with the thermos inside. Oh, how they loved those days and choosing their favorite characters for those lunch boxes! Michelle also received dresses, as girls were not allowed to wear jeans to school in the 1970s. That took a tremendous load off my shoulders. Now I just had to house and feed my kids.

A few years later, my sister Janet moved in with me after graduating high school. She worked in the grocery store and paid her rent in fresh fruits and vegetables, the much- needed food group I had not been able to afford for my children. She brought home random items of food that had been marked down or sold at discount right before the expiration date on the package. Before Janet's arrival, we lived on Kraft macaroni and cheese and hot dogs. The kids called it Mac-Mac, and still do to this day. I know how unhealthy these foods are today, but if you invited me over for Mac-Mac and hot dogs, I'd be there in a minute. It remains comfort food, just not as healthy as my mother's kidney bean salad or my own salmon with dill sauce.

Today, I have become quite the cook, and my husband, Kevin, brags to his friends about the fresh gourmet dishes I prepare. It's so nice to be in a loving, caring relationship where the money worries are shouldered by two. A team is a wonderful thing to be part of, and Kevin is the partner that Fate dropped into my life.

On the tenth anniversary of Damon's death, his sister, daughter and others left beautiful messages on her Facebook page. I'd like to share these words with you from those who knew Damon...

A message from his daughter, Morgan:

Exactly ten years ago to this day, I lost my role model, my partner in crime, and most importantly, my dad. The man who was supposed to watch me grow up, scare away boys, and one day walk me down the aisle, left this world much too soon. Every day I miss him, and although it's been ten years, he will always be my daddy... Although this day is hard, I just wanted to acknowledge how amazing of a father he was and how glad I am that I had him in my life for as long as I did. I love you, Dad, and I hope I've been able to make you proud, as you have been watching over me all of these years.

His sister, Michelle:

Okay, I have been trying to write and things keep getting in the way. I must have needed more time to gather my thoughts. Your dad wasn't just my brother; he was my best friend growing up. There are so many things he's missed in the last ten years. My heart still hurts that he is gone and I cannot share my life with him. He loved you so much, Morgan, words just aren't enough. You were his squid and ankle biter, his little buddy whom he cherished with every breath. I know that he's watching you grow into a beautiful, intelligent woman with a quick smile and a generous heart. I still tear up when I think of him being gone.

I have lots of memories though that helps me keep him close. I always knew that if I had nothing else, I had him. We had crazy fun times and fights over stupid things. Laughed at the hamster in the plastic ball running around the house. Rode bikes to the library and turned the shed into a fort complete with power and a cot. He played Dungeons and Dragons and built Lego cars with the intent of building one that could survive a trip down the stairs. The 6 Million Dollar Man (action figure) didn't survive his trip. His "bionic" legs fell off! We shared music and books and friends.

I "borrowed" his flannel shirt so many times he bought one exactly like it and gave it to me for Christmas. At least I know that when he left us, he was in such a happy place in his life. He liked his job and was planning on getting engaged. He had the greatest friends ever. Most of all he had a beautiful daughter that he loved very much. I love you Morgan. (Damon was last seen in a plaid flannel shirt and jeans of his mother's choosing…his legacy).

Dear friend and longtime roommate, Margit:

Thinking of you this weekend, Morgan. Love you. Miss him. He is so proud of you. You have become such a beautiful young woman. I would give anything to meet him for a beer and listen to him tell me why his kid is so much more amazing than other kids, LOL. I have spent the last hour typing this and deleting and typing again trying to find the right words to tell you how I feel. I suppose words just aren't enough. You are always in my heart and forever on my mind.

Margit's Mother:

Morgan, all of us in the Jensen family miss him so. What a lovely thing you wrote about him. You were by far the most important person in his life. We all feel a great loss by his absence, but of course you would feel it much more as he was in your life every day. I always enjoyed going down to visit Margit in California and enjoyed him so much. He was wise beyond his years. All of us miss him so.

Dear next door neighbor, Dawn:

Where to begin? Damon became one of our best friends pretty much immediately after we moved in next door. Over the short period of six

It is I, Amadeus

years, he came to be like a brother to me and was often mistaken as Mike's brother (Mike is Dawn's husband.) *when we went out. He taught me to truly appreciate a meal (3-4 courses and at least a 2-hour process). His sweet daughter, Morgan, and I share the same birthday.*

We'd watch TV in our PJs sometimes (walking next door was not so far, right?). He understood the important stuff – true friends, quality time, and caring less about "the Jones's." He was quite the chef, made fabulous truffles, and was there for you no matter what. Even the last Christmas that my Grandma was going to be alive, I couldn't be there because of the flu. I sent Mike over and was miserable on the couch. Who shows up? Damon. After Xmas with his family, he came over to stay with me & didn't care that I was sick. He parked himself in his usual spot – on the floor with the sliding glass door to his back. That's the kind of guy he was.

We vacationed together – I remember him borrowing your van, Frances, that all of us (Damon, Mike, Barry, Lisa, Cristina & I) would fit. When I had Jake, he sent a basket full of sweets to my floor so that I got hooked up in the private room. After we had 2 weeks bonding time with our baby, he insisted on babysitting so that Mike & I could go out to dinner. We came home to him asleep in the recliner with Jake on his chest. He was a great dad with Morgan, and knew just what we needed. Like a brother, he (& Barry too, his best buddy) had a great time teasing me when I was pregnant & especially at the thought of me having a boy (since I'm such a girlie-girl).

He stayed up until 2 a.m. listening to my disappointment after driving my alleged dream car and finding out the BMW wasn't my "ultimate driving machine." We enjoyed countless BBQs and really, it was pretty funny watching how excited he and Mike would get over knives. Both great cooks, they competed in who had the latest and best knives. My black lab, Onyx, was nick-named "Angus" after she got so overweight... from Damon & Barry throwing Milk Bones over the fence to her all the time. I can still hear his laugh as he & Barry fessed up to it.

I was so happy that he had met someone that was perfect for him. We all loved Sarah.

When I'd buy him a nice shirt for Xmas, he'd say, "You keep buying me clothes just like my mom."

"Well, you can't keep wearing the same flannel shirt or that faded burgundy shirt, Damon!" I'd tell him.

Ten years ago today came the shocking phone call that changed everything. He was supposed to meet my new baby that I was going to have in a month. He was supposed to watch and guide his beautiful daughter as she grew up. He adored her and was so great with her. We were supposed to go through the "comparing notes" stage as we and our families grew older.

As I've reflected over the last week about my dear friend, Damon, I am so thankful that God blessed us with you in our lives. Those six years were much too short, but we built a lifetime of memories. How rich we are to have had that gift of time with you. We miss you tons and love you forever, Damie-D.

"Damie-D" was Damon's never-to-be-forgotten nickname. Thank you, Dawn, for the memory!

Chapter Four

Fate Brings Kevin to Me

It is I, Amadeus. Yes, we brought Kevin into your life. He is filled with love and is extremely happy to bring your children along on his journey. He will give you untold days, weeks, months and years of devotion. Lucky you!

With love, Amadeus.

Over the ensuing years, I visited numerous psychics and read stacks of books on the spiritual realm. One seer told me that the man I was dating (who shall remain nameless) had blue eyes and was a Scorpio. That was completely true! She added that "Scorpio" had a son who needed him greatly. Yes, he was divorced, and his son was the most sensitive of his children, so that was also true. The son lived in Phoenix with his mother and siblings, and his daddy was only a weekend dad.

Scorpio moved to Phoenix, and when he invited me to come with him without marriage, I knew that I could not put myself and my children in that position of uncertainty, so I declined. My job at that time was a solid one, and my family support system was in place in Tucson. It was a difficult decision, but once I'd made it, I began to look for a home in Tucson to purchase. I had my real estate license, but was working as a bookkeeper in a commercial real estate office, and my boss graciously agreed that if I purchased a home, she would return my entire commission to me, even though she was entitled to keep part of it.

I didn't have the $1000 down payment I'd need, and I'd never borrowed money before (or since), but I submitted the following proposition to my father: If I could borrow $1000 for 30 days, I would repay it out of my commission. He agreed to help me, and I became a homeowner. It was not an easy journey, purchasing a home as a single woman in the 1970s. I had signed the deed of my previous home over to Steve when we divorced, and it was written that way in the divorce decree. Steve let the home go into foreclosure, and it showed up on my credit report. Now at the mercy of the bank, I was blessed to meet a woman loan officer (very rare in the 70s) who brought the divorce decree to the bank's mortgage approval meeting – and, miraculously, I was granted the loan I needed! The money was received from my employer, repaid to my father, and he was able to repay the bank, as he'd had to borrow the money to share it with me. I will be forever grateful for his love and generosity.

In April 1975, I met Kevin Patrick Pullin. He came to the real estate office where I worked to pick up the keys to a store for which we were trying to find a new tenant. (The company that owned that store employed him.) We chatted and he flirted, but at that time, I was still dating the Scorpio, albeit long distance.

Kevin and I met again a year later, while out for drinks on a Friday night in April 1976. I was with friends, and he was with a group from work. Kevin was employed by a convenience store chain as a Field Consultant and would often entertain out-of-town company employees. This was another of those nights. He asked me to dance after chatting and reminding me where we'd first met. We enjoyed several dances, and I had a fabulous time in his arms. He called me the next day at my office. Since I was no longer dating the Scorpio, I accepted his invitation to dinner the following weekend.

Kevin and I continued to date through the fall of 1976, and I felt such a strong feeling in my heart that I knew I was falling in love. He was the kindest and most considerate man I had ever dated. He was punctual, which was and remains important to me, and loved many of the same things I did! We dined in nice restaurants, went to movies, and enjoyed the company of each other's family and friends. I introduced him to my children, Michelle and Damon, who were enthralled with his laughter and warmth. Kevin comes from a family of six children who enjoyed teasing and laughter, and my sister, Janet, gave her immediate stamp of approval. She was living with me at the time and watching from the sidelines as the four of us interacted.

By the end of the year, Kevin was invited to join my parents and siblings for Christmas dinner at my parents' home, where his warmth and conversation skills won their hearts, along with my sister and brother. He has a way of putting other people at ease by getting them to talk about their lives. He was filled with questions for each member of the family, which nudged them into their own comfort zone.

That Christmas day had dawned with a new puppy – Kevin's gift to the children. He had asked my permission first, and we'd gone to the kennel the previous day to pick up the little black-and-white mixed breed that needed a home. We hid the puppy at my parents' house and snuck over very early to bring her home in a cardboard box. The children were so excited that they could hardly wait to leave Grandma and Grandpa's home and return to the delicious kisses lavished on them by this darling pet! She was promptly named Cindy by Damon and Michelle, and they loved her and her slobbery kisses – until she ran away and found a new home. I know there's a dog at Damon's side on the Other Side and wonder if it's his beloved Cindy.

I kept teasing Kevin about asking me to marry him, and he always responded by saying he had a specific life plan: First he had to have a good job, a home of his own, and a reliable car, and then he would date his prospective bride for two years before popping the question. He had accomplished the first three and was closing in on the fourth. Of course, I am a much less organized soul and was already eager to say yes!

Finally, in September 1978, Kevin was ready to commit to our future, and on bended knee, he asked me to marry him. I was moved to the depths of my soul. I knew that age was on my side, and that this wasn't a silly, hasty marriage. This was the real deal. My soul mate had asked my hand in marriage, and I couldn't contain my joy! We'd been dating just shy of two years, but Kevin had been transferred to Pomona, California, earlier that month, due to a promotion, and knew he did not want to leave me and my children behind.

Sweet Damon, when told of the upcoming marriage, couldn't stand the excitement! "Can I call you 'Dad' now?" he asked. He was ready for a new adventure! Michelle was more cautious, as that is her way. She was old enough to know that if her mother married someone else, there was no chance her parents would ever reconcile. She, too, loved Kevin, but she also knew that our marriage meant moving to California, away from everything that was familiar. Family and friends would be left behind, so the experience would not be a highlight in her young life.

Kevin had made a commitment to us, and he took it very seriously. He and I drove to California to find a home to buy and put our Tucson homes on the market. At the time, there was a serious real estate boom in Tucson, as IBM had opened a new facility and was transferring their employees to Tucson from California. Imagine selling a home in California and buying in Arizona – a move that's great for your investment portfolio, but not so great when you give up balmy California for the Arizona heat! Most of the IBM employees were buying more than one home, so it wasn't long before our Realtor called and said she had a client who wanted both our properties – and included in the price they wanted the refrigerators, stoves, washers and dryers. We were selling to an investor who wanted great rental properties! I was thrilled, as we were headed in the opposite direction, and the cash we took with us enabled us to settle into a cozy, four-bedroom home in Claremont, California.

On October 28, 1978, I married Kevin Pullin, who is still a part of my life today, and who stood by my side as I entered into classes in the psychic realm. Not believing, but not standing in my way. He is a wonderful, caring person and was put in my life to stand beside me for many years and trials. We moved to our new home immediately after the wedding. And so it was that I would leave the town where I grew up and head off into the world, taking my two children, Michelle and Damon, with us.

After two years, Kevin was transferred again, and he took us to Bellevue, Washington, which is across Lake Washington from Seattle. It is there that we settled down and had two children, Kevin II and Sean, and where Kevin adopted Michelle and Damon, raising them as his own alongside our little ones. Michelle and Damon's birth father, Steve, was in the Navy and out of touch for long periods of time. Steve agreed to the adoption and signed the necessary documents. We went into the judge's chambers on a gray, rainy day in Seattle, and after signing our documents, the judge requested that Kevin and I wait outside. The children were asked if they were in agreement with this adoption. They were now in their teens and had to agree, or it would not become a reality. They did, and with love and abandon, they became Kevin's children. They loved their stepfather, and we were now a family with one last name! A lovely lunch at the world-famous Pike Place Market was enjoyed by all of us in celebration of this new family dynamic.

It was also in Bellevue that Damon, ever the character, rode his bicycle down the steepest hills, breaking his arm twice. He and Michelle joined the ski club, where they took lessons every Saturday for years. Damon became one of the daredevils who were allowed to leave the group, build jumps, and ski in uncharted territory. He loved the excitement of flying through the air, just as he had on his Big Wheel – that magical cycle with one large wheel in front and two smaller ones in back – so many years before.

It was during this time in Damon's life that we noticed that he befriended those who needed special attention. His inner circle of friends were polite and kind, but often in need of family life, and they found just that in our home. Our doors were always open, yet some of them feared me, as they knew I was a no-nonsense mother. They'd tiptoe around for the first half-hour after their arrival – before they relaxed enough to let the fun begin! Each of them felt like part of our extended family. Many are still in touch with us today and remain our loving kin.

Once, during a trip across the bridge to Seattle, I was told by a psychic that my youngest son, Sean, is part of the Lost Children of Atlantis. She said that Atlantis and Lemuria used to be part of the North American continent, but were covered with water and now lay deep in the ocean. Eventually, Sean himself confirmed this for me.

I do know that Sean is extremely sensitive and psychic, but chooses to ignore it. I believe, though, that the more I become involved in things spiritual, the more he may, too. For example, I recall that every time we attended a baseball game for his brother, Kevin II, I'd ask Sean if the team would win or lose – and 95 percent of the time he was correct! I remind him to this day to listen to his intuition and to act on it, as he is always receiving information from his Guides on the Other Side. It's a reminder for me to listen, too.

Of course, I can urge Sean to listen to *his* guidance every day of the week and still not remember to listen to my own. When I catch myself not listening to messages from my Guides, I smile, knowing that I am still a student in this field of metaphysics. But even if I don't always listen or remember what I'm told, I'm always deeply aware that my Guides love me and are with me to help me grow spiritually.

Once, during an award trip to La Costa Spa in Southern California with some members of my husband's company, I visited the resident psychic. When she asked what I really wanted to do with my life, I told her I wanted to become an interior designer but added that a friend had gone into this business and I did not want to appear to copy her. Ever insecure, I was letting my insecurity rule my life, and I was not following my heart. Her sharp retort was, "You've not a moment to lose!"

Soon after our visit to the spa, Kevin got a promotion from his company and was transferred to Southern California. I was distraught that we were moving and leaving Damon and Michelle in the Bellevue area, as they had flown the nest and would not be coming with us. We moved to a new home in the city of Orange and made it our own, tearing down wallpaper and putting up new. Arranging furniture and paintings on the walls was part of my therapy after leaving Damon and Michelle behind. It saddened me so much – even though they were now 18 and 20, I felt they were just babies and still needed me. At their age, I was already a mother and could not forget the stress of that time in my life, when I was in Tucson and my parents were living in California.

Michelle was pregnant with Devin, and I would miss the activity surrounding that blessed event. She was unmarried and I felt that her safety net was moving away when she needed it most. Another thing that troubled me was that my dear friend, Linda, who had stood up for me as my Matron of Honor when I married Kevin, had transitioned July 4th of that year. As I attended her funeral, plans were already in place to have the movers come into our home and begin packing. Shattered, I arrived home to find a wonderful, caring man packing my kitchen into boxes, answering the telephone, and fielding calls for me. He was the best person ever in the moving business!

Once the new home in California was in order, the children – Kevin II was 7 and Sean was 5 – started school, and I found myself alone and engulfed in deep sadness. I did not have Damon and Michelle close by to nurture and had left lovely friends of eight years in Bellevue. Since I no longer had the wonderful group of Bellevue mothers to share my days and stories with, the telephone became my friend as I made long distance calls for companionship. I finally pulled myself together and began to volunteer at the local elementary school. Coming out of this darkness, the school became my new home away from home, as there was always something there to keep me busy.

A neighbor invited me to a join a group she belonged to that raised funds for Providence Speech and Hearing, a well-run facility in Orange, California, that does hearing tests for both those who cannot pay and those who can. (That's just the tip of the iceberg of what that wonderful facility provides to those in need of their services.) But nearly four years of belonging to the Villa Park Chapter of Providence Speech and Hearing, with two years as president of the organization, found me on mental and physical overload. After all, I was still raising two children, working at the elementary school, and taking care of my husband. I decided to end that tenure and move into other things, as being president of such a wonderful group was time-consuming. No question that it was rewarding, too, but I was ready for a new adventure – design classes at Santa Ana College!

That year, Damon followed us to California and lived with us for a time. He entered college to study culinary arts and worked two jobs.

He married, had a beautiful daughter, and divorced. He remained in California, and we spent many wonderful days and evenings together, cooking for each other and the family. We enjoyed many happy hours watching his daughter Morgan swim in our backyard pool. She clung to her daddy, and he clung to her. It reminded me of how he'd hung on to his sister to ease his pain during my divorce. His love for Morgan was so apparent. They played games for hours in the water, and still she could never get enough.

After many years alone after his divorce, Damon had begun a relationship with an enchanting yet level-headed woman, Sarah, and planned to marry her one day. Our daughter, Michelle, was still in Seattle. She had not joined us, but remained up north, where she gave birth to her son, Devin. However, when Devin was two years old, I received an unexpected call: Michelle was ready to leave both Seattle and Devin's father. I knew that if she moved to California, she would have difficulty getting a place of her own, with the price of apartments so high and daycare for Devin to worry about. I suggested she call my mother, as she was all alone in a big, three bedroom house in Tucson. My father had passed away the previous year, and I knew that if Michelle moved in with her, Mom wouldn't be lonely anymore. She could care for Devin while Michelle worked, and their presence would banish the lonely energy in the house.

Meanwhile, I met Donna, who became a dear friend, through the children. We decided to attend interior design classes together. I had almost completed my studies when my husband's job was eliminated, and he had to accept a position that paid less money. So now I really *had* to find a job – the psychic at La Costa Spa had been right! She had predicted this new career path, and now here I was in search of a job in my new field with "not a moment to lose"!

My interior design instructor informed me of a position with a furniture company, and I knew that if I could sell myself to them, I could sell their furniture. I interviewed, was offered the job, and accepted it! That was the beginning of a seventeen-year career in interior design.

Chapter Five

A Vacation Like No Other

It is I, Amadeus. This was a vacation like no other. You brought your family together to rejoice in each other. You were not aware, as we were, that these would be indelible memories for each person who laid their head to rest in your vacation rental.

Continued love, Amadeus.

In August 2003, many family and friends gathered for a week's stay in our rented seven-bedroom house at the beach in Newport Beach, California. It was a fun and sun-filled vacation with those we loved. But as Damon and his girlfriend, Sarah, left on Saturday night to attend a wedding and return to their home in Studio City, I felt a catch in my heart. I sensed that Damon was ill and noticed a tiredness and puffiness as I straightened his tie.

I have had many intuitive feelings in my lifetime (ignored some and followed others), but this one was too difficult to wrap my thoughts around, so I decided that the long week in the sun had been draining for him and let my anxiety rest. Looking back, I believe I was being protected by my Angels from knowing what was to come. That evening, Damon left his daughter Morgan in our care, and we took her home to her mother, Kandace, the next day. Damon and Kandace had divorced before Morgan was one year old. It was sad, but not for me to judge or change, although I did try to change it more than once. It was, as I have since come to understand, a lesson they had agreed to learn in this incarnation on Earth. I now believe that the journey for each of us is written and agreed upon by all parties before we arrive on this planet.

Six weeks later, on a Sunday afternoon, a fire was raging in the forest above Rancho Cucamonga, California, where Morgan, now eight, lived with her mother. I called Damon and asked him to call his daughter.

"I feel she is fine," was his reply.

"I want you to let her know that you are not in any danger of fires in *your* area," I told him. He did make that call, which was to be Morgan's last conversation with Damon, and mine as well. (I guess I was listening to my Guides and Angels that day when they suggested I call him). He left us that Sunday in the darkness of night.

The following day, "Grampsy" (my husband, Kevin) and I went out to Rancho Cucamonga to help Kandace break the news to Morgan of her daddy's death. I stared at my husband in shock at his suggestion we do this, not realizing that it *was* my place as Morgan's granny and Damon's mom to be with her at that moment. My grief was so strong that all I wanted was to hunker down at home and nurse it, but Kevin, steadfast and true as always, was teaching me yet another adult lesson. This was the saddest, most gut-wrenching thing that I have ever had to do in my life. Who says growing up is easy?

A decade later, Morgan and I continue to keep a journal whenever she visits, writing down memories of her daddy so that one day she will be able to share them with her children. I know I would not have her here so often or know her so well if Damon was still with us, as she spent many weekends with him without us around. Also, her mother was dating now, and relied on us to be with Morgan. She has become Damon's gift to our family, and we love her unconditionally. I now know more than I did before about her relationship with her dad – like when they went to the grocery store, if she could count the change back to him, she could keep it. In clever ways like this, that child of mine had grown into an outstanding father! Now a bubbly teen, Morgan laughs at how, before every birthday party at our house, she and her dad would

It is I, Amadeus

make a frantic stop at the store for a gift and a card on their way over! Little things like this are being recorded forever through the journaling that takes place in my kitchen – and now through this book.

Since Damon's death, we have never returned to the beach for a week of fun. That family tradition is suspended in time. But perhaps one day I will plan a new vacation there with the new additions to our family tree.

Chapter Six
My Spiritual Journey Begins

It is I, Amadeus. Greetings this day, Sweet One. We are going to introduce you to many who have contact with my "world." They surround you, but you were not aware until you stepped onto this new path.

Love, Amadeus.

Strangely, right before Damon's passing, I was at a time in my life when I was surrounded by psychics. In fact, the Thursday before his transition, I was helping a co-worker, Barbara Anderson, who had purchased a home from the company we worked for, design countertops for her new kitchen and bathrooms when she became extremely agitated. Then, for some reason known only to her, she confided that she was a psychic.

I was elated! The group of women I worked with was very spiritual, and they had brought me quite far on my spiritual journey. We were all longing to meet a psychic we felt comfortable with. I immediately went into the back office and spread the word! There was much hugging and excitement, but then I had to go back to work. When I came back into the studio, Barbara pulled me aside. "I see a shadow of a man at your right shoulder," she whispered, becoming very distressed. Then she looked away for what seemed like much too long and suddenly asked *if my father had passed*. I told her he had. She quietly said that it must be him that she saw.

Needless to say, questions raced through my mind. "A seer is supposed to know *who* is standing at your shoulder," I thought. And even though Barbara seemed fairly certain it was my father she saw behind my left shoulder, I sensed somehow that the message might be a bit askew. When I told my husband, he agreed. "I do not feel that your father is watching over you," he said matter-of-factly. Kevin doesn't believe in any of this "psychic stuff," and he knew my childhood years had not been easy ones. So I decided to take what Barbara had said lightly, without any further investigation.

In the ensuing years, I have found that my father really *is* at my side. He has apologized for any parenting mistakes, and I have happily forgiven him and openly embraced his soul. Over time, I have come to realize that our loved ones often learn beautiful lessons on the Other Side as they continue to work on their souls – in fact, my parents have become exactly who I wished them to be when they were alive. Today, they support me in all that I do, and my mother has even asked to help finish this book! I have acknowledged that she is welcome, and my dad sits in love watching over me. They tell me of their love and how proud they are of me each time I connect with them. And my son, Damon, and brother, David (who died in November 2012), tell me through Spirit that they hang together and enjoy fishing.

When Damon transitioned the Sunday after Barbara shared her vision, I knew it was him she had seen that day in the studio. She may not have known his name, but she knew it was my son that she saw. Of course, a loving psychic would never give you that kind of startling information. It was only after the funeral that Barbara confided that it was Damon she had seen that day.

Damon's body was cremated, and his urn is resting at Fairhaven Cemetery in Santa Ana, CA. A plaque on his niche reads: "His soul had been released to move lovingly among us." It was me, his mother, who wrote those words. They came so easily, and yet I anguished over using "among" or "amongst" in the text. I quizzed many people, and they looked at me with sadness and said, "It doesn't matter." But, it *did* matter. It mattered to me! I was his mother! I was writing, I thought at the time, significant words that spoke to the meaning of Damon's life being cut short at such a tender age. It needed to be right, and I screamed inside my head, demanding perfection for this last gift to my son. I had a deadline to turn in the information, so the plaque could be fastened to the wall where his ashes would be placed, and so, at some point, I simply gave up my struggle with the two words. I chose "among," and "among" it will be for all eternity.

The chapel at Fairhaven Cemetery overflowed during his service. There was standing room only, as so many had been touched by his sojourn on this Earth plane. They had come to pay their respects and to say their goodbyes. At the luncheon in our backyard after the service, people who'd known him on his journey came to celebrate his life. Family and friends came from all over the country and found comfort in being together. Stories flew through the air, and between the laughter and tears, a newly-formed group celebrated Damon's life.

The funeral passed, the family and friends departed, and I began the slow trek to my unfamiliar new normal.

When I came back to work, my co-worker, Barbara, sadly confirmed that it was Damon she had seen that day in the showroom. She knew he would be crossing soon, but the information she had downloaded had shaken her to the core. She had been so profoundly affected by her ability to tap into such knowing that she'd closed it off for a brief period to recover from the shock

After the Christmas party at the design center, Barbara asked if she could talk to me about Damon and give me a message she had received from him. I was delighted and quickly agreed! (She is still one of my favorite people, with her infectious laugh and love of life.) Barbara is not only psychic, but she's also a medium. A psychic has the ability to read the energy of another human or animal and give messages based upon it; a medium has the gift of seeing, hearing, or sensing the energy of those on the Other Side and bringing messages from them to us here on Earth. With the protection of the White Light from above and the Angelic Realm, these messages are given with love for those left behind when a loved one transitions into the Light. On the spiritual path, you may choose to just be psychic, or you may add the ability to be a medium as well.

As Barbara described a room to me that Damon was showing her, I could not believe my ears! The room had bookcases, "something hidden," and bean bag chairs. She said that Damon was telling her all about it, as it was in his favorite home. My goodness! She had just described our home in Claremont, California. The room was the den, which had once been a bedroom. One wall and one partial wall held beautiful, dark wood bookcases, and bean bag chairs sat in the middle of the room for Damon and Michelle to lounge on. If you pulled on the short side of the bookcases, they opened up into a hidden space that had once been a closet.

That area was unique, to say the very least – a hiding place for kids and things you didn't want everyone to see. As Barbara described this room, my spiritual beliefs were unquestionably confirmed. Damon's spirit lived on! I could communicate with him through psychics and mediums, but I have since come to know that I can communicate with him myself at any time, day or night. I ask him questions and he answers. He also sends messages of love to everyone I am in contact with who knew him.

That day, Barbara also described a Christmas ornament Damon was showing her – and as she spoke, she looked up to find one exactly like it hanging from the company tree right above her head! Damon was telling her that he'd tried to put it on our Christmas tree when he was young, but a man in the room was angry and didn't want him near the tree.

"Who is this man?" Barbara asked.

"It's the man who is no longer my husband," I replied. Steve had died of a heart attack many years before Damon's crossing. Barbara then explained that Damon wanted me to know that he was searching for that man, his birth father. Damon wanted to know why Steve had created a situation that ended in his leaving his family. I will remind you here that I have learned that these situations are agreed upon before we incarnate into our bodies. With that emblazoned in your mind, you'll see why I believe that my marriage, children, and subsequent divorce were all part of lessons to be learned. That is what I've been taught by my teachers and through the books I have read.

I'm comfortable with that concept and invite you to ingest it and see if it resonates with you. I have chosen this belief for myself, and it helps me sort through the unhappy memories of my relationship with Steve. Through this knowledge, I have been able to remember the happy times and the joy of becoming a mother to Michelle and Damon. Without that relationship, they wouldn't be who they are today. Their souls may have still been born to me, but their experience of living, first with Steve and me and later with Kevin and me, unequivocally influenced who they became.

I had another reading with Barbara many weeks later, but this time we were in her home. Whenever she reads for me, I always give her my wedding band to hold, as it has rarely left my hand for over thirty-four years. With the energy from my body etched into the ring, she has an easier time connecting to my personal energy.

She has had many messages from Damon and fascinating insights about my other children. She told me that my son, Kevin II, would ultimately marry his girlfriend Amy. That has happened, and we love having her as a part of our family. Barbara also let me know that my son, Sean, was not dealing well with the death of his brother, and that his relationship with his girlfriend at that time was not a solid one. She saw that he needed more motherly support than either he or I knew. Yes, this situation was, in fact, occurring, and it took Sean moving home for his heart to begin to heal. Some of Barbara's insights have come to pass, and some are still waiting for time to pass so that they might unfold.

Chapter Seven
Psychics Become a Part of My Life

It is I, Amadeus. Your journey is not what you expected all those years ago as a child at your mother's knee. You were with her and she put beautiful braids in your hair. Her true job was not known to her or to you. You have traveled far on your journey, and she sits on the Other Side and is filled with pride of you and your accomplishments.

In love, Amadeus.

Over time I got to know the sister of one of my co-workers, Lisa Garabidien. She has been psychic since she was a child, and has developed her gifts to become a healer. She and I had a session, and I loved many things that she told me.

During her first reading, I was told she saw a contract with my name on it, and it was true that I'd been looking for a new place to work, as I felt stifled where I was. The company had instigated rules about our designs, and I found my creativity crushed in the process. A few days after the reading, I attended a staff meeting and had an uncomfortable feeling in my gut. You know the one – that gut instinct that tells you something is about to happen, but you can't put your finger on it? Well, following the meeting I had a call to go to Human Resources. I looked at my teammates and said: "This is it. I am being let go!"

As I sat in a chair across from the manager of my department and the HR manager, I saw a contract with my name on it. It was my pink slip. That was the contract that had been seen! I was laid off and couldn't contain my glee, as now I could search for new employment without the burden of hiding it from those I worked with. The spirituality I had learned from my teammates made me feel dishonest when I was looking for another job while still employed by this company.

In 2006, this woman began teaching classes in spiritual development and invited me to get to know my psychic abilities with her guidance. We began with meditation and automatic writing.

As I explained earlier, while meditation is meant to calm the mind and get you in touch with the Source, automatic writing is when you journal what is being shown or told to you by your Guides after the meditation is complete. At times, you will write automatically when a question you have in your mind is answered by a Guide or other entity that is helping you during this lifetime. It's through this education with this teacher and my many other teachers that this book has become a reality.

I enjoyed the classes, even though I felt that I was an infant compared to everyone else in class. Some of the other students had already been working on their meditation and writing, and they had such wide-eyed wonder and excitement about what they were learning and seeing during meditation that I felt I was just sitting on the sidelines. I didn't see what they saw by any stretch of the imagination, but I was beginning to read other people's energy and trust what I was receiving from the Other Side. When I use the word "beginning," know that I do not use that word lightly. It took many years to completely trust what I was receiving and to act upon it. I have had many lectures from my Guides during my automatic writing to teach me to trust. At this time, I trust what is sent to me via writing or telepathically. I have come a long way in the past seven years. As my story continues to unfold, you will witness this growth and see the person I have become.

The most important thing that I have learned is trust. Trust is being taught to me by my Guides and Angels, who chat with me after my meditations. They were vigilant until I mastered self-love and trust in all they were teaching me. When I stumbled, they would chat with me through many means and put me back on track. They continue to remind me to trust to this day, as it is easy to stray off a path you have not walked before in this lifetime.

As I listened to others in that first class, I learned buzz words and phrases that are used by people in the spiritual community. Now that I was aware of them, I began hearing them more often. The cleaning lady at the company I went to work for after being laid off was chatting with me one night, and when she dropped the word "Source," I asked, "Are you psychic?" She affirmed that she was indeed! Another day, I was having a lively conversation with my hairdresser, Marge. I had just begun to patronize this salon again and asked where the owner was. I had been a client years before, but had switched to another place closer to work. Now I was back, and in answer to my question, Marge stated simply, "The owner has crossed over."

I immediately knew that I was in touch with another psychic-minded person, who I now call a friend. She had used the words "crossed over." You will note that, in this book, I use "transition" or "died" in its place. No word or combination of words is right or wrong – it's just that we often avoid the word "died" in everyday conversation. I've used it in this book, however, for your ease in reading and understanding. If you are a beginner on your journey with spirituality, you will soon have many new words added to your vocabulary; and if your journey began long ago, you'll recognize these words and remember a time when you, too, had to learn them. Those of us who have begun working with our Guides and Angels know that what many call "death" is just the soul leaving the Earth body to travel to another dimension where we can still communicate with it.

At work one day, a sales rep was talking quietly about her automatic writing. She described how her handwriting changed from its usual tidiness to scribbling she could hardly read. I was astounded. I had made another psychic connection! Days later, I was telling another sales rep about this woman I knew in our design field who did automatic writing.

This rep said the other woman's name out loud, but her intonation made it sound like a question. I asked if she knew her. "No, I do not," she said. "That name just came into my mind unexpectedly and I blurted it out without thinking!"

She'd had a psychic "hit." For no reason she was aware of, the information had just come to her, and I felt that this happened to continue to teach me about the path I had chosen to take. I had many lessons to learn, and this was one of them – that we psychic-minded and spiritual people are everywhere, even in the most mundane places! We are typical people, going about our daily lives and reaching out to each other. You may find, too, that like-minded people will show up to guide you into trusting your decision to continue to develop spiritually.

I continued to grow in the classes, and one night in class, another student received a message that I have at least nine Angels and Guides around me. It was quite surprising that someone I hardly knew would receive a message for me that would be relevant. What I needed to know was that I should not stop when I knew one name of a Guide or Angel, but continue to discover others.

Today, I know the names of many of my Guides, Angels, Fairies and others. There is Amadeus (I call him the "boss," as he is the first Guide who came to me and continues to bring in more messages than the others). Amadeus is my Master Guide. He answers psychological questions to help heal others and brings general information for my growth. After meditation, with pen in hand, he writes with me more than any of the others. And always, depending upon my question or dilemma of the day, the needed entity steps forth through my writings to give me the advice I need.

Chapter Eight

Meditation My Way

It is I, Amadeus, Sweet One. This is a chapter that you have been longing to write and longing to get others in your circle to understand. As long as you calm yourself through meditation, or any other way, you will be able to clearly hear your Guides, like me and Others. Enjoy writing.

Love to you this day, Amadeus

It is I, Amadeus. Greetings this day, Dear One. You meditate and you practice what you have been taught. You must be tough with us and instruct us to step back and leave you in peace so that you can clear your mind. When you wish to meditate deeply, you must send us away. We are so excited to chat that we forget to respect your quiet time. Forgive us and send us into silence while you calm your mind. Continued love, Amadeus.

My belief concerning meditation is that one does not have to burn incense, light a candle, sit in a special position, or cross your legs – though you may choose to cross them or to lie on the floor instead of sitting. You do not have to be barefoot, nor practice rituals. You must just be in the moment.

This is your journey, and this is your choice. I'm asking you to be sure *you* make the choice to meditate and are not pressured in any way to follow the actions of others. Be with Source Energy, or whatever it is you would like to call it. Depending on your religious background, you may call this energy Buddha, God, Allah, or whatever feels comfortable to you. I have decided, for the purpose of this book, to call this energy Source. I believe that name to be universal and without judgment or connected to any particular religion or belief. I am not here to judge anyone. I only wish for you to feel grounded and safe in any belief you personally choose that feels right for you.

During meditation, some people cross their legs and sit on the floor. Others feel the need to place their hands in a special position. Do not judge anyone about how they sit in meditation, or for how long they choose to remain in that state. Some grounded souls feel the need to meditate for extended periods of time, but that may not be right for you.

Not judging other's paths is the *one* thing you must do, for we are all on our personal journeys with unique lessons to learn. Let me add here that if you do not connect with another's energy, you may choose to put distance between you and them, but that doesn't mean you are judging them; you are simply choosing the energy you wish to have in your life. You will know what is right and what works for you.

As you move into spirituality, you may want to give up the rules and practices learned in the church and give power back to yourself. If this is what you want, you have picked up the right book! Weigh this choice heavily and decide for yourself if this is the direction your life will be taking at this time.

You've been drawn to this book to enjoy its content, and if a book or subject draws you to it, then it contains information you are supposed to know. You may not immediately know the reason why that book fell into your hands, but it will be revealed to you eventually, and when that happens, you'll sigh in wonder at the synchronicity of the Universe and it will bring a smile to your face.

I have never felt so much love for myself as when my Guides and Angels work with me. They ask that I love myself without judgment. They ask me to trust in the Universe and its Divine intervention. I am guided to trust in them as well, and, most importantly, to trust in myself. I have learned that my Guides and Angels are with me always, and knowing that I am not alone on this path brings such serenity. I have trusted these entities to teach and guide me toward love of self. Anger, anxiety and frustration occur much less often as I continue my spiritual journey and acknowledge the lessons I have learned and will continue to learn.

As we proceed ever onward through this book, I will teach you of meditation, as I know it, and the calming effects it has on the mind and body. Take a moment right now to close your eyes, sit or lie down, and breathe deeply and slowly. Hold your breath before you exhale. Slowly take another deep breath, hold and exhale. Do this three or four times, relaxing more with each breath. Sit quietly, concentrating on the slow movement of your chest as you breathe in and out. Try to settle the mind from the thoughts of the day by just thinking of your breathing. Once you have taken those initial breaths, your breathing will become soft and slow, and you almost feel as if you don't have to breathe at all!

Continue to relax and know that this is the beginning of meditation. If you have soft music, you may want to play it quietly and listen to it with all your attention. This will help to clear your mind. Many recorded meditations guide you to a peaceful place in a meadow or forest. There you may hear a babbling brook and take a seat on a rock or a beautiful bench nearby. There are many ways to meditate. Choose the one that feels right for you.

Do not be concerned if you cannot quiet your mind easily. Practice each day until it becomes easier and you relax and journey out into the Universe in peace. You may have noticed that I said above, "As we proceed." By this I mean that I am with you on this journey. I, too, evolve more each day as I listen to my Teachers, Guides, Angels, and all Others who are with me on this path.

A meditation does not have to last for hours. Sometimes just one minute will bring you the relief you need. Typically, ten or fifteen minutes stolen from your day will bring you to a place of calm and reverence for the energy that is you. And by the way, if you've ever missed your highway exit and thought you were daydreaming, that, too, is a form of meditation. So relax, unwind, and know you can do it – because you already are!

You may want to do chakra clearing during meditation. Chakras are vortexes within your energy field. The main ones begin at the tailbone and end at the top of your head. Here are the seven primary chakras and the areas of your life they affect:

The Root Chakra is the color red and is located at the tailbone. It impacts career, grounding and survival. During some meditations you are guided to see the Root Chakra go deep into Mother Earth and connect with Her core.

The Sacral Chakra is orange, located in the pelvic area, and impacts relationships.

The Solar Plexus Chakra is yellow, just behind the stomach, and corresponds to your self-esteem. This is where you might feel knots or anxiety if there is a pressing problem to be solved in your life. It is here that you get a "gut instinct" about someone or something, and you need to stop and listen to what you hear from this instinct via your Guides and Others.

The Heart Chakra is green and in the middle of your chest. This chakra is connected to loving and empathic relationships. You will feel a sense of gratitude when connecting with this energy center.

The Throat Chakra is bright blue, located in the throat area, and governs emotions and communication. It's related to speaking your truth. Here is where the Guides and Others speak their truth.

The Third Eye Chakra, located between the eyebrows, is purple and assists you in making intuitive decisions. This chakra will open wide as you learn to use it more and will bring visual information into your mind's eye.

The Crown Chakra is lavender and located at the top of the head, blending the purple of the Third Eye Chakra with the white light that connects you to Source. Your messages from Source and Others come through this chakra. By opening it, you open yourself to hear what is being told to you to share with others during a psychic reading, or what is told to you during your journaling.

The chakras run in a straight row up your body along the spine. It only takes a moment to clear them and see their beautiful colors. They are spinning vortexes, moving slower at the bottom and faster as you go up toward the crown.

During meditation, if you desire to clear your chakras, begin by breathing deeply and slowly. As you blow the breath out, picture the color of each chakra. Next, envision white light coming from above your head from Source and blend it with each color. Do this by visualizing the white light joining the chakra color and seeing the chakra begin to spin. Begin with the Root Chakra and continue through all the chakras until you reach the Crown Chakra. When you've done this, you will have achieved a complete chakra clearing.

As you practice this exercise, you are now beginning to balance your body and mind based on these seven energy centers that govern all your organs and work together, both independently and as one system.

I've given you a brief overview of the chakra system and you can find many books that describe in detail what you can do to keep your chakras clear and strong, thus giving you more control over your own energy. Some teachers use different colors for these chakras, but what I've set forth here makes the most sense to me. Do you sense a pattern running through this book? My approach is always to take what I want and leave the rest, and I implore you to do the same – with this book and others. This is a principle that I especially want you to learn: Be your own essence. Be true to you. Do the work and decide what resonates with your soul.

I do suggest that you meditate at about the same time each morning or evening. If you wish, keep a spiral notebook or leather-bound journal and pen beside you, so you can write down any messages that may come through. Here's how to do that:

At the close of your meditation, take three slow, deep breaths, then open your eyes. Now, write whatever comes into your mind at that moment. Do not pass judgment on what you write; just write. This is how I came to know the Guides and Angels that I will introduce to you in this book. When I began meditating, I made it a practice to date the writings in my journal, and that's how this book evolved. Later on, you'll find messages I received from my Guides, Angels, and those on the Other Side.

Meditation is a basic tool. It will give you many hours and days of bliss, once you have mastered it, and even a few minutes of doing it will give you great peace. It need not take long. If you are feeling tense at work, close your eyes, breathe deeply, and go inside to calm the energy within and around you. You may even take time in your car during your lunch break to just be with you and with Source.

Often, I just close my eyes and breathe slowly for a couple of minutes, and that's all it takes for me to connect with the Source energy. Oh, the notebooks I have filled with the writings that follow! Usually, the messages I receive are for me personally, unless I have asked for help for another. That is how easy meditation, followed by writing, can be.

But you don't have to write. If you choose to master meditation and never write a word, follow your heart and do just that. Each person finds their own way. At first, I thought I had to be still for hours, but my Guides explained that if I was to do that each day, I would lose interest and not meditate at all. So find what is right for you. Know that at times you may wish for a longer meditation, as I sometimes do. If so, take that time. Own it. Go within and lose yourself being with Source.

It's true that there's work to be done on the spiritual path, but you will find much joy in both the process and outcome. I particularly enjoy running into like-minded people on this journey. When I worked in the design centers, sometimes I'd hear a catch phrase like "crossing over," and I'd know I was in the company of a psychic soul who was practicing – not denying – the sixth sense. Still, in the early years of my spiritual growth, I was not always ready to commit fully to that which was unknown to me. Little did I know that I was being pushed in the direction of finding my life's work and my path to oneness with Source! The push was ever so gentle, and I moved slowly, reading everything I could find about meditation and devouring books on the subject of spirituality.

You will, at some point, if you choose to proceed on this part of your journey, meet your Guides and Angels and feel their energy, as they are with you always. Sometimes this manifests as a tingling in your hands, fingers, and/or at the top of your head at your crown chakra. This is a sign that these harmonious energies are here for you. They will teach you love of self, which was the first lesson my Guides and Angels wanted me to know.

Through meditation and automatic writing, you will hear messages and write them down. You will hear specific information that is being given to you by your Guides, Angels and others on the Other Side of the veil. When you read what you have written, you may see words that have never been part of your vocabulary, but there they are on the paper! These words have been given to you by an entity on the Other Side. They are bequeathed to you to guide you on your journey, and to let you know that you have actually connected with one of your Guides or Angels, or with others who love you unconditionally. If you ask for a name, they may give you one. This can take time or be instantaneous. Just trust what you are hearing in your mind. These entities do not need names on the Other Side, as they recognize each other's energy. When they come to you, however, they know that you need a name, for that is how we recognize each other on the Earth plane.

Your Angels and Guides will be specific about the information they are giving to you. Listen, and do not judge the experience. Time is needed to perfect this process, and to feel the love and beauty of this life experience. At first, you may want to edit or question what you are hearing and/or writing, but move ego out of the way and quit editing what you hear. Just accept the communication. It takes time to learn to trust this information, but once you accept it, a new world will open to you.

Even if you had an enchanted upbringing, most of us are not taught to love ourselves. As I raised my four children, I did not know to say the words, "Love yourself as you love me." There were passages in the Bible I studied, but I didn't make the connections that I make now in my spiritual life. Now that I have entered this harmonious spiritual place, I am able to tell my children of this love, and I've been able to teach it to my granddaughter and grandson as well.

I want to close this chapter by talking about protection. We all need to ground ourselves when working in this realm of spirituality. When writing or channeling, I know that I am surrounded by those who love me and that I am completely protected by their love. There is no need for the ritual I was taught about surrounding myself with love, light and purity for eternity and letting only those who love me enter into my communications. This ritual is fear-based, and since I am not in favor of rituals, I have taken this one out of my tool-box and replaced the fear with acceptance of the love surrounding me.

Yes, there is dark energy. You will learn to recognize it through what you are taught. Keep yourself in love-based energy, and surround yourself with white light. Envision tree roots coming from the bottom of your feet, going deep into Mother Earth and wrapping themselves around Her core. If there's no time for that, hug a tree!

Chapter Nine

The Last Piece of My Puzzle

It is I, Amadeus. Yes, Dear One, your life is a puzzle. You may not have thought so ten years ago, but you will agree it has become one. You are surrounded by love and light. We will be with you as long as you are here, and perhaps in your next lifetime.

Love, Amadeus.

At the suggestion of my friend Lynn, I visited a well-known medium in Southern California after Damon's transition. Tim Braun hears and sees those who have crossed over and brings forth their messages. Tim is a gentle spirit with a warm voice, polite and a gentleman, whose smile puts you instantly at ease. In short, he's amazing! I spent a delightful hour with him and was so at ease that I returned for another session after my mother crossed into the Light.

My first visit with Tim was all about Damon and what he was accomplishing on the Other Side. Contrary to widespread belief, we do not rest once we return to the Source. We continue to work on our lessons, just in a more peaceful and benevolent atmosphere.

Damon spoke through Tim by giving him information telepathically. He explained that he had been faced with a choice to go to the Light suddenly in the middle of the night, as he had, or linger on Earth and become hospitalized. He told me, through Tim, that his choice had been to not burden his family and friends with trips to the hospital in Los Angeles, when his death was inevitable due to his heart's compromised condition. It's comforting for me to know that even in his passing; he was still the loving, caring man we knew him to be. And, just as he'd wanted, we did not make long trips to the hospital to sit at his bedside in anguish, only to await his transition at age thirty-three.

Damon showed Tim a certificate that signified he had finished his degree in Culinary Arts. He'd been working on this degree before he got caught up in the task of making money to support his family, which consisted of Morgan and her mother, Kandace. He was so proud and flashed a grin as he displayed the certificate. Then he asked me not to be so sad, as he is always with me. He sent his wish for me to tell his brothers, sister and father that he loves them and is with them always. I have a recording of the session and listen to it every few years, just to relive the first time I heard from him through Spirit.

During my second session with Tim, Damon was joined by my mother, who had crossed over the previous year. Tim stated that my father was also with them, but sensed that he did not want to talk. Now, that was not like my father at all! It had been over twelve years since he'd transitioned, so he may have become a changed man, but during his incarnation with me, he could talk for hours and loved to!

At this second reading with Tim, the spirit of a woman who'd had cancer came through, but I could not place her at that time. Tim said her name sounded like "Carol" or "Carolyn." I'd briefly known a woman named Caroline who had transitioned from cancer, but after leaving the session and mulling it over, it dawned on me that it was Colleen! She had recently transitioned from breast cancer, and when I spoke with my Guides later that week, they said that Colleen wanted her children to know she was doing well and laughing heartily again. Before leaving Earth, she had become weak and pale, and the laugh she was known for had waned. I found a friend of the family and asked her to pass Colleen's message on to her children. I suggested to this friend that the children might enjoy visiting Tim and hearing their own messages from their mother in Spirit. I don't know if these children ever contacted Tim, or even believed that they could receive messages from their mom. It's possible the idea may have frightened them, but I do hope they enjoyed knowing that Colleen is happy and laughing again, as always.

My mother asked me that day, through Tim, to "give her love to the girls." That would mean my sisters, Marilyn and Janet. Janet had turned her family room into a private room for my mother, when she lived with Janet and her husband Barney in Tucson. My sister became an incredible caretaker, seeing that Mom had good meals, clean laundry, and got to her doctor appointments on time. Janet was always there if Mom fell, making sure she was carefully lifted back into bed, even if she had to call the paramedics to assist. Marilyn lives in Denver, but she arranged her work schedule so that she spent many days – which added up to months, over the years – in Janet's guest room, doing what she could to relieve her sister from some of her caretaking duties. I did not help with the caretaking, except on rare occasions, as I was living in California and working grueling hours. I had little time off to take the eight-hour drive to Tucson, and knew that if I did, it might upset the schedule my sisters had so beautifully orchestrated.

My mother then thanked me for my kind words, and for being with her when she crossed. Many of us in the family were there as she left for the Light. But it was I who held her hand and gave her our blessings for her transition, to ease her on her way. The journey had been a long one, and it was time for her to be free of pain, humiliation and frustration.

During this session with Tim, Damon gave me a beautiful red rose for taking care of his daughter Morgan, and gently laid it on my lap. (No, I did not have an actual rose in my lap, but that was the gesture Tim described.) I do take care of Morgan with love and without obligation. I wouldn't have it any other way.

After that, there were other messages for family members from both Damon and Mom, channeled by Tim, and soon a birthday cake was cautiously placed in my lap. Tim and I determined it was for me, as Tim said it was a late May or June birthday. My son Sean has his birthday in June, but mine is the 23rd of May. The medium made the decision it was for me when he announced there were "many" candles. Thanks, buddy!

My mother wanted to acknowledge that she was part of the gift of the birthday cake, as well as Damon. I laughed and thought about the many birthdays she'd missed in my adulthood. My mother's intention was to always remember our birthdays and special occasions, but she would often procrastinate over addressing the card and mailing it. There was plenty of proof of that when we moved her from her condo to my sister's house and threw over one hundred greeting cards into the trash! Some had been signed but never mailed, and her love and caring were felt through that stack of "almost mailed" cards.

Later that day, when telling my sister Janet about my visit with Tim, she reminded me that it was a few days before my birthday when Mom passed. Now, she was delighted to be saying "Happy Birthday" to me and sending a "gift." My mother would not have been able to speak those words on my birthday, had she still been on Earth; nor could she have purchased a gift, due to her many disabilities before transition.

While the sessions with Tim were fascinating, I had no intention or desire to study mediumship. I enjoyed these other-worldly chats and knew Tim had an unusual gift that helped my heart mend somewhat. But I had not yet begun my spiritual journey, and so it never crossed my mind that this was something I might come to do years later.

In 2012, Debra Hookey began teaching mediumship classes at the School of Multidimensional Healing Arts and Sciences. Enthralled by my spiritual journey, I toyed with the idea of joining her class for some time. Could I really learn to do what Tim did? Could I really help to heal others, as he had helped to heal me? Debra's class didn't fit into my schedule, as I was taking other classes on Thursday night, so I loped along for a few months, and finally decided to ask my Guides if I was meant to learn this modality. Their answer was emphatic: Yes, they said, this was "the last piece of my puzzle."

My puzzle? I didn't know there *was* a puzzle. What did that mean? Nonetheless, the message was clear: These Guides who love me without question were telling me to begin my journey into this modality. In fact, as soon as I could, I finished up the other classes I was taking, my schedule cleared on Thursday nights, and I found myself in Debra's class. The

Universe was orchestrating my new direction! And so it is that I began my mediumship class.

During class, I give and receive many messages. We constantly practice, and Debra's mantra is trust, trust, trust. One evening in class, as we exchanged messages, I heard from my father, who said that one lesson he'd learned upon his return to Source was to talk less and listen more. Knowing that we continue to evolve on the Other Side brought a smile to my face and gentle tears to my eyes. I loved hearing this message and knowing that he has learned to listen to others and hear what they have to say. So many hours of my young life were spent listening to hours of his incessant rhetoric as he taught me right from wrong.

As I advanced down the road of spirituality and added mediumship to my plethora of modalities meant to heal physical and mental pain, I came to understand the importance of spirituality as it relates to me personally. In order to relay messages from Spirit, trust is the key. As my Guides were teaching me to trust what I hear when I channel and to write down the messages or speak them, the same information was being taught to me in Debra's class. She, too, insists that we trust what we see or hear, and to relay that information to our clients. So now I have evolved into a medium, as well as a channel, and see that these two similar skills have made my journey complete. The last piece of my "puzzle" has been put into place.

Chapter Ten

Learning Through Living Life

It is I, Amadeus, Beautiful One. You have so many lessons to learn in this lifetime, and you are tackling them with precision and love. You have learned that a home and yard are not the awards you are here to earn. You are learning that life is a constant, changing journey. You are doing an exemplary job!

Love, Amadeus.

Kevin and I sold our home of countless memories in 2008, the house on Modoc Street in Orange, California. Poignant memories of Sean and Kevin II growing up, Morgan diving for toothpicks at the bottom of the pool, Damon at the grill, and Michelle bringing her son, Devin, for visits from Tucson, have all been catalogued in my mind.

We sold the house because it was much too large for just two people, and with Kevin II's marriage, the emptiness had become unbearable. Kevin II had never left home, and we missed his sly sense of humor, his sarcastic, off-the-wall comments, and his kitty cats that were part of the family. His love is unconditional for those he allows into his energy.

My youngest son, Sean, has taught me that we take our memories with us, as a house is just four walls. Sean has the uncanny ability to find the right words at the right time and sense the needs of others.

Frances Pullin

He pointed out that my desire, at that time, was to justify this move by saying I needed a change. I needed to heal in peace from Damon's departure in unfamiliar surroundings – and he was so right!

With visits from Sean, Kevin II, Michelle, my husband, my granddaughter Morgan, and extended family and friends, Kevin and I now are now enjoying our new home in Anaheim Hills (only a few miles from Modoc Street). And when Michelle comes to visit, I appreciate this home more than ever, as she and I are making loving memories here for both of us.

Michelle and I share so many "Damon memories." We make chocolate chip cookies for "Big Bird's tummy," the Big Bird cookie jar given to me by my mother when the youngest boys were toddlers. It sat for years on my kitchen counter, constantly filled and emptied with a vast array of delightful nibbles. When Morgan was born, I gave it to Damon, who used it for various cookie-making extravaganzas.

Michelle and I cook and laugh together. Her laughter is as contagious as that of a baby playing peek-a-boo, and is ever-present in my mind. She teases me about how I let the younger boys get away with things she and Damon never dared do – like jumping on the bed, which somehow is now okay with me. We laugh about the times when, as kids, they made cookies but weren't allowed to use the oven without their dad or me in the house. She's confessed how, when we were away, they would make two batches of cookie dough. One was eaten raw by the two little cooks, and one was scooped onto the cookie sheets to await her dad or me coming home from work, so they could be baked under parental supervision. So many stories, so little space to write them all here.

Today, loved ones gather with us on all kinds of occasions to create more memories. Morgan has grown tall, intelligent and beautiful, as her daddy knew she would. I know that, from the Other Side, he has watched her grow into a stunning 18-year-old college student.

When she was younger, she visited often on weekends, and on one of our shopping trips with Grampsy's wallet, she picked out a comforter and shams for the guest room. For a few years it was pink and green and little-girly, but in her junior year of high school, her visits became less frequent, and I converted her room to a yellow floral theme that matched the antique bedroom furniture we inherited from Kevin's mother. Many friends and relatives have visited over the years, and now the house has become a home.

And oh yes, as time has passed, I have learned through my spiritual training that Damon is with me and knows just where I am! He is often present at readings in class, and in my daily life. I have learned I can write with him and channel him. The spiritual work I'm doing now has brought him closer to me; today, he's no longer beyond reach.

Kevin and I will move again, but never will it be as tumultuous as when we left the house on Modoc Street, which held many untold stories now embedded in my mind. After all, as Sean says, "A house is just four walls, and you take the memories with you."

Chapter Eleven

Synchronicity Visits Us All

It is I, Amadeus, Sweet One. I am with you this day to guide you through the telling of the family's synchronicities as we have collectively, on the Other Side, orchestrated them. These are places in their lives where they are able to choose to go forward with an event or to reject it. Wishing blessings for this family's journey together.

Love, Amadeus.

In an earlier chapter, I talked about fate bringing Kevin into my life and how it changed the future of my children and me. In this chapter, I'm going to develop that concept, sharing some of my family information, along with some amazing synchronicities. These so-called "co-incidences" occur in all our lives, but once you begin to suspect that many events are orchestrated by the Universe, you'll be able to accept this concept or reject it. I have made it a practice to note in my journal the times when the phone rings and the person calling had come into my mind only moments before. This happens often, and it has helped me to trust myself and what I know and am hearing in my mind. This is the trust that has been asked of me so often by my Guides.

When a student arrives at the school for a class that is scheduled the following evening, I ask, "Why are you *really* here?" Then we take a look at the roster for that night and invariably find a class that fits exactly what the student sensed they should delve into in the near future. Just another example of how "chance" provides an opportunity for higher learning!

At this point, I'd like to mention some of the synchronicities that brought my children and their spouses together. These excite me, now that I'm on my spiritual path. In each case, it was their "destiny," and they accepted it, though I now believe that we can change the energy of our destiny, should we wish to.

Our daughter Michelle and her husband Nick met in Tucson when her son, Devin, was a youngster. Devin's father had returned to Seattle about the same time Nick was stationed in Tucson with the Air Force. Michelle had never married Devin's father, and her move to Tucson had been without this man. One Saturday night, Nick and Michelle found themselves alone sharing a drink, and since they were both without partners and discovered they enjoyed each other's company, they began a relationship. They dated for a few years and were married in an outdoor ceremony in Tucson. Nick had been married previously, and his children from that union, Cody and Samra, along with Devin, rounded out their family. Thus Fate entered the lives of my daughter and her son, changing them forever.

Kevin II, my third child, is married to Amy. Amy and Kevin II got to know each other when their high school German club took a summer trip to Germany. Amy was in her sophomore year, and she and Kevin, who had just graduated from the same high school, discovered young love as they meandered through the streets and pubs with their German teacher, as a guide. Kevin had been eyeing Amy during their German Club meetings, but was too shy to chat with her. Then Fate intervened. As a recent graduate, he qualified to go on the field trip to Germany, and when the Universe presented this opportunity, he finally found the courage to approach Amy. Thus began a long courtship that, many years later, culminated in Kevin II's marriage to Amy on June 7, 2008, in Costa Mesa, California. An uncanny twist: They got married on Amy's parents' wedding anniversary!

My other son, Sean, met his wife Lauren at a party, and they were instantaneously struck by each other's laughter and mutual love of music. Lauren was in college in San Francisco and in town for the weekend to visit her parents in Orange, California. They sat beside each other and talked and laughed into the wee hours of the morning. Ironically, they each decided silently to themselves that a relationship would be "geographically undesirable" and that it wouldn't make sense to even begin dating. So they returned to their respective schools without each other.

After completing a semester abroad, Lauren returned to Orange County to finish college – and a coincidental meeting though mutual friends brought Sean and her together again! This seemed like the right time to get to know each other, and Sean courageously asked Lauren for her phone number. They began dating and found each other to be loving, adventurous and respectful of family, friends, and, most of all, each other. They dated for four years and were married in Orange, California.

Chapter Twelve

Stepping onto My True Path

It is I, Amadeus. You have stepped out of the shadows and onto your true path. Enjoy its rewards!

Love to you this day, Amadeus.

It was in October 2009 that I started a channeling class in my home. Channeling is when a person puts ego aside and allows an entity from the Other Side to come through their voice box with messages. I had two regular students and didn't charge them for the class. I felt that since I was still a novice at teaching, I would practice with them, and they would take what they wanted. One of them, my friend Donna who attended design school with me, is still close and I give her books to read, as she is seeking knowledge of spirituality on her journey.

I held these classes on Monday night, and my husband, a non-believer, would go upstairs at 7 p.m. after saying hello and visiting with the ladies. He would then ignore us completely. He knows I love what I do and is pleased to see me happy in the wake of things that had brought such sorrow to my heart. By this time, I had abandoned the classes with my teacher at the school due to time restraints, cost, and the burning desire to try teaching on my own. The student was ready to fly! Know that you will do the same. When that happens, honor those who have taught you and move forward. When I start teaching someone who is just beginning to experiment with their intuition, which is innate in all of us, I bring up something that most of us can relate to. I say, "Did you ever put a glass of liquid in the refrigerator without a lid on it, and something told you not to? Did you ignore the thought and do it anyway? Then, later in the day, did you open the refrigerator, spill the liquid, and reprimand yourself because you hadn't listened to the voice inside?"

That's a great example of what I'm trying to get others to understand, and what I'm still learning myself: Listen to that voice. The voice inside loves you and does not want you angry at yourself and on your knees cleaning up spilled liquid! You have many Guides, Angels, Fairies and others surrounding you with love. These adoring entities give suggestions whenever they can, and if you listen, they will help you in your daily life. Your Angels are just waiting for you to ask for help and truly cannot interfere unless you ask them for assistance. These entities are also asking you to love *you* and believe in *you*. You are being asked to trust that the Universe is perfect, in spite of a bad day or horrific news reports.

In September 2010, I was invited by an acquaintance, Serafina, to rendezvous for lunch. I readily agreed, as I had met her while taking classes with my first teacher and found her to be a joyful being. As I came to know Serafina, I was astounded at what she already knew about archangels, ascended masters and the multitude of saints she continually referred to. There was not a moment spent with her that I did not revel in her company. Serafina had been in class the night Amadeus made his presence known to me in 2007. She was so supportive of the discovery of this Guide of mine that she'd giggled until tears filled her eyes, and I thought we both might create such chaos that we would be asked to leave the room! The other students just stared dumfounded at our antics, and we knew we needed to quiet ourselves and return to silence.

At the time we met for lunch, Serafina was working at the School of Multidimensional Healing Arts and Sciences (SMHAS) in Laguna Hills, where I was to meet her. I arrived in my usual timely fashion and was introduced to the owner, Jerry – and that meeting changed my life forever.

Serafina asked me to channel, and so it was. Amadeus came through me with answers to a variety of questions that she and Jerry asked, and they were both visibly pleased. Later that afternoon, Serafina and I lingered over lunch, planting seeds about how I could start volunteering at SMHAS and we could enjoy each other's company on a more regular basis.

After returning to the School with Serafina on that life-altering afternoon, I conferred with Jerry about how I could fit into the structure of the organization known as the School of Multidimensional Healing Arts and Sciences. The two of us agreed that I would volunteer one day each week, beginning the following Tuesday. In return for my time, I would not have to pay rent for a room where I could teach my classes and begin charging students a fee.

It was then that I knew I was ready to begin my next step into the reality of who I am in this spiritually-minded community. I am a channel, a psychic and a teacher, and on that afternoon, I was on the verge of accepting payment for my gifts and my teaching skills. Much earlier on my journey, I'd heard rumblings about not charging others for my gifts. Those rumblings were silenced when I learned that these gifts are valued by others, as well as respected. If people don't charge, and just give away the information, they're viewed as not having as much experience as those who charge sizeable amounts of money. It validates me, my gifts with the value I place on them.

I eagerly began volunteering at SMHAS and found myself surrounded by like-minded people! It was the perfect place for me to finally start teaching others the baby steps of meditation, automatic writing, and channeling. It was not long before I was volunteering two days a week, instead of just one. I needed more time in that exhilarating energy of like-mindedness. As I volunteered my time, I became a familiar presence at the school. People who came to teach or study knew that I was there to assist them and to greet them with warmth and comfort. I would check them in and show them around. Many of us have formed unbreakable bonds.

As I worked alongside Jerry, he introduced me to his concept of turning the school into a co-operative organization. In November 2011, I was offered a position on the co-op board and a portion of the school's revenues, once it began to turn a profit. I accepted and am now a member of the Co-op Board at SMHAS. That makes me a part owner and gives me a heightened sense of responsibility to the school and all who enter there. I know I am not there forever, but it has given me the perfect place to study, learn and practice my rediscovered natural abilities of psychic knowing, channeling and healing.

Jerry, as the founder of SMHAS, began the school believing in Divine guidance. When he felt it was time to move the school to a new location, he called on the Universe for more of that guidance. Pendulum in hand over a map, he located a building for us in Irvine, California, comprised of small rooms we could use for classes, and a room big enough to house around fifty guests for larger lectures and classes. In 2011, this became our new school. Everyone is much happier in the new space. I have been with the school for more than three years and consider myself a permanent fixture.

Today, we're continually growing, featuring teachers, students, and videos on our website! Our first open house was May 1, 2011. As a partial owner, I couldn't be prouder of what has been built in three short years. Plus, I am now a respected teacher, and wish to bring my teaching to you. I can't believe where I have been taken on my journey!

When I teach a class or do a channeling session, I am in awe of the love people get from me and give to me, as they embrace me with abandon. I give them a gift of love and light, and they return it immediately. Spirituality is such a loving emotion to embrace. There are so many modalities that I cannot begin to name them all, as new ones appear in the school each week. When any person is in integrity with what they are teaching or doing, the love that flows is phenomenal! These days, many exceptional practitioners and teachers are discovering the school and enjoying the energy they find there – and the students are finding us too! It's a magnificent sight to behold, this school, and so rewarding emotionally to be a part of it. I am a permanent fixture, so look for me and say hello when you join us for a class or event.

It is important for you to know that SMHAS is an all-volunteer organization at this time, with people eager to get involved knocking at the door at a steady pace. We do this to keep costs low and classes affordable, and we hope to keep it this way. It allows volunteers to receive a discount on their classes, which provides them the opportunity to take even more classes for their personal growth.

I wish for all to join me in this delightful community of spirituality of which I have become a part. You may not be able to attend this wonderful school where I am volunteering, but you can join me in spirituality wherever you are and whenever you choose. There are facilities similar to this center all over the world! I ask you to find one, if you are so moved. If you can't find a similar school, tap into our online classes at www.smhas.com.

We hold a Faire at the school on the last Saturday of each month, where visitors can attend free lectures and sample different modalities. Many seekers come for readings to satisfy their curiosity regarding their futures. Some receive healings from practitioners who have the ability to offer healing energy for physical pain or to heal the soul. Many stay for part or all of the day, waiting to chat with anyone who will discuss the spiritual realm or share something new they have learned, felt, or seen. During the free, thirty-minute lectures that go on all day long, guests have the opportunity to learn about a new class or a different modality. It is there that I channel, and the audience asks questions which are answered with sage, loving advice from my Guides – usually Amadeus.

Channeling is wisdom from others who once walked the Earth plane. These entities enjoy teaching this wisdom with their words. They have learned their lessons, but remain on the Other Side and love giving back to those who will listen to them through channeling or automatic writing. Not all of the seekers who receive answers in a channeling session are pleased with what they are told, but I cannot be burdened with those who are displeased, as it is not me who is giving the sage advice. That advice is given by the entity using my vocal cords, and the truth that comes from my Guides is not always what a person wants to hear. Thus, the client may have an unpleasant reaction. Still, it is always with love that these messages are brought forth.

One Saturday during a lecture, Amadeus was fielding questions from the audience and a young woman wanted to know the name of her Guide. Amadeus told her he was not privileged to bring her that information as she would personally have to do the work it would take to discover the name. She was disgruntled by his answer, but I have been taught by my Guides, Angels and spiritual teachers that if you don't do the work to shift your mind from judgment to acceptance, you will never stand in your own spirituality. Thus, in my own spiritual journey, I have learned to trust the information my Guides bring forth, and these teachings that come through me. It is my hope that one day, this woman and all seekers on their spiritual journey will learn of the love of their Guides, Angels, Fairies and Others. This love has helped me be able to look in the mirror and witness love of self looking back at me – one of life's most fulfilling experiences. The following quote was given to me by Amadeus to remind all of us of the time it takes to find this love of self:

It is I, Amadeus. It is during this past ten years that you have learned that God is just a name put upon the Source from which you all came. You are strong in your spirituality and in reverence to what you have learned. Go forward and love yourself as you love Source. Love, Amadeus.

Chapter Thirteen

Knowing Source

It is I, Amadeus, Sweet One. You have come so far on your journey, and we are pleased with the success you have made in recognizing the Truth in what we are teaching you. We are beyond excitement with the Truth you are teaching others. Thank you for this.

Love, Amadeus.

I have come to understand, through my reading and studying, that all that is in the Universe is energy. I have an understanding that we are all part of that energy called Source. We all have the same energy coursing through us as the plants, trees, animals and sea life. We are born from the energy of Source for an Earth plane experience to teach our soul many lessons. These lessons were chosen by us before we entered the Earth's energy field.

Those who believe in this energy give it a name, such as God, Buddha, Source, Energy, Higher Power, but it does not matter what name you use. What does matter is that you believe in the energy and respect and love that it is real, and that this energy is with you always. We do not ever leave this energy, even upon our transition, or what many call "death." The name "God" is what I was taught to call energy before I began to believe that by being a piece of Source Energy, I am also the Source. It's difficult to envision this concept because it goes against my childhood religious teachings. But when I leave behind those teachings and embrace this new concept of belonging to the Source, I feel joy and blessedness. This I have done with my conscious mind.

The first time I heard someone say, "I am God," I was stunned. It came from a dear friend I was working with, Donna (a different Donna than the one mentioned earlier). Donna and I worked at the same design center as Barbara – the psychic who'd sensed that Damon would transition – and was part of that very spiritual group of women in that company. We've had many long chats, Donna and I, about this bold, thought-provoking "I am God" statement, and I now know these words to be true, because I've questioned my Guides and they've confirmed it. I do not mean that we are Source Itself, but rather that each of us is just a tiny particle of Source energy. We are created from Source, and we return to Source upon our death. It does not mean when we accept that we are Source energy we are all identical. We maintain, in each lifetime, a personality and traits, formed in the womb, which make us unique

Donna, raised Catholic, and I, a Methodist, knew we had to leave many of the rules of the church behind when we embarked on the spiritual path. But we did not leave behind the teachings in the Bible – they just took on deeper and more substantial meaning. By "substantial," I mean that I have much more understanding and awareness of these age-old spiritual concepts that have been taught through time.

Through years of study, I've also come to understand that we travel in soul groups, and that members of a group often reincarnate together for soul lessons. We decide before we are born if we will incarnate as a male or female energy, based on the lessons we need to learn during our next incarnation. We also decide – with the help of a Council on the other side of the veil – who will be our parents; and we decide the many other paths we will take through life to achieve the lessons we want to learn.

I chose my parents and the family of sisters and brothers I grew up with, and we all took on each other for personal reasons. For example, I now know that I chose my mother to help heal the timid feelings embedded in her family's DNA, and to bring strength and courage to the women in my lineage. My Guides have helped me to know this through the automatic writing I have done. By revisiting my past lives through past-life regression, I found I had been a victim and have come into this life with untold strength. My spiritual work has healed that part of my DNA and also healed many women in my linage stretching backward in time. Thus, when they reincarnate, they no longer bring lack of self-confidence with them, but enter instead with strength and courage. I also know now that we pick the day and time that we are brought forth into this world. That is why astrology readings are often so accurate.

So next time you hear the words, "You can choose your friends, but not your family," take a moment to rethink this. You definitely choose *both* your family and friends, and you do that before you incarnate. As you have chosen lessons to be learned, you have also chosen how to learn those lessons and with whom. Of course, you can deviate from that choice, as you always have free will. How is this possible? Because the psychic is reading your energy, not pulling things out of the air. It's *your* energy that prompts them to say what they are hearing or feeling during a reading. So, if you change your energy, the reading will change.

Know, too, that you can also change the outcome of a reading from a psychic when you are given information that you do not resonate with. Change the energy within you, and you change the outcome. For example, if you hear from a psychic that you are going to get a new job in six months, but it doesn't happen, re-examine your thoughts at the time of the reading and compare them to your thoughts today. Perhaps things shifted at work, and you no longer dislike where you are. Why would you want to change jobs when you are happily committed to your current one? You and you alone, can change a reading, knowingly or unknowingly. Do not blame the psychic for being wrong; instead, examine what's in your own energy field.

If you have already found your inner sanctum, these words do not frighten you – they simply reinforce your beliefs. If you are just beginning your spiritual journey, you will and should question these words. In meditation, ask your Guides and Angels to help you with these concepts. I honor your right to do this and hope that you will. If you don't, then you are a victim of acceptance, wrongly thinking that because

Frances Pullin

these words are written, they must be true. Know that you are being asked by me to explore the potential of this information and question what seems too "out of the box" for you, just as I questioned the phrase "I am God" that a co-worker spoke. I'll go into this more as we proceed; at this point, my goal is to fill your mind with questions that compel you to seek answers. I am a teacher, and to be good at what I do, I need to excite you – even aggravate you at times. Know that through the love I emanate, you need not be frightened, but just curious instead.

Part Two

Chapter Fourteen

The Journey Continues

It is I, Amadeus. As your journey continues, you will discover the truth in who we are and how to trust in those of us who come to you with unconditional love. We come to love, protect and nurture you. You have learned to listen, and that will continue, without doubt, throughout your lifetime.

Love, Amadeus.

As the untold beauty of the day unfolds before me, I continue on my spiritual journey of writing this book. Sharing the message of spirituality brings bliss to my soul, knowing that you, too, might enjoy what it is that I know and believe to be the truth. I accept this knowledge as truth, as spirituality has happened to me and through me, and I am in complete trust that the gift of spirituality was meant to be known by me. I know, too, that when my son summoned the courage to give up his life here on Earth and return to the Other Side to share the bliss of that space with others, he set me on the path of my pre-ordained destiny.

Do I have trepidation about my transition, or what some call "death"? Yes, but only because it revolves around knowing that my passing will inadvertently cause pain to all who know and love me in this current lifetime. I know that I'm going to a place of bliss to be reunited with all the souls I hold close to my heart, and that I'll treasure that moment, but I'm also aware of the sadness felt by those left behind on the Earth plane. Damon put it so well when, during one of my sessions with medium Tim Braun, he sent this message: "Though the hurt is not intentional, the grief when someone transitions to the Other Side is felt by the soul who has left."

Before we make our transition, we think that we will not see the future wedding being planned or the child who is yet to be born. But as Spirit, we see all of these things, as we are able to move lovingly among those we care about. The difference between being in our Earth body and in Spirit is that not everyone recognizes that we are with them in Spirit, once we have crossed over. And we are no longer in physical form and able to hold tightly to our loved ones who have remained on Earth for the duration of their contract.

This message of Damon being with me always has been told to me by many mediums and psychics, and I have written his words as he sits with me and communicates telepathically from the Other Side. My mother, father and son are now together there, and were joined by my younger brother, David, in November 2012. They have all told me through direct communication that they are with me always, assisting in my journey. My parents, without the stress of their lives on Earth, have become the parents I always imagined they could be – understanding, loving and supportive. I longed, throughout my life that they would be those loving parents, and now I thank them for who they were then, and are now, without judgment or prejudice.

I know that my channeling is the journey I am here to experience as I continue the work I've done in past lives to learn soul lessons. During those lives, there were often dire consequences for this type of communication with the Other Side, but in this incarnation, there is no penalty of death for knowing and sharing all that I know and all that I am shown. And this time, I'm remembering many things from my past lives and life on the Other Side that take me further on my journey, until it is time to join my son and others in the Light once more. In this life, I'm recalling how to listen to the voice within and follow its directives, as well as communicating with Spirit through my meditations and journaling.

A reminder: There are many parts of this book that are being "channeled" through me. Now, if that is a new term to you, know that it was new to me at one time too. Let me remind you once again of the nature of that information, so that you understand its origin.

To recap: Channeling is a process where your ego steps aside and you allow those from the Other Side who have had past lives on the Earth plane to come through you in thought or in voice; or you allow Angels to speak through you and share information that comes from their capacity to know all. (Angels have not had an Earth experience, according to what I have been taught). Guides come through, too. These are typically souls who have traveled on the Earth plane, learned their lessons, and now guide and teach.

Many say that it's enough that we have a "Higher Self" who's with us always, and that's all we need to tap into this guidance and information. I respect their position, and since I'm a channel who brings forth many entities, I also include my Higher Self in that group that speaks through my mind and voice box. I believe that the term "Higher Self" describes an eternal, omnipotent, conscious and intelligent being: You.

I will tell you that, at this time, my passion is to channel. Whether I'm channeling while I write, talk to groups, or am helping another soul heal in this lifetime, I love what I do. The love that surrounds me while doing this work is incomparable to any emotion I have felt in this current incarnation.

When I write after meditation, I consider that channeled information. The messages that came through at first surprised me, as they contained words I've never used. Now, however, those words have become so familiar that I'm no longer amazed by them. Channeling takes extreme energy, and I sometimes become very warm. When I channel, meditate, or do any of this work with a group, the group raises the energy higher, just by being in the room. The energy moves even higher as my Guides and Angels gather close, along with those of the audience. Then, much to my joy, the energy increases even more as many loved ones who have crossed over join in. This amplified vibration brings everyone in the room into a safe and spiritually-connected state of being.

The entities who come through me, when I invite them, answer inquires about themselves or about things going on in the questioner's daily life. Different entities come through, depending on the type of question asked. For example, when I meet with a person who has medical or mental issues, Mother Theresa comes with her quiet presence and loving advice, sending gentle words through me so the soul can begin to heal. I always make a recording of the session so the questioner can listen to the message over and over again.

As you get into this work, you will learn that this relationship with your Guides, Angels and Others is for your personal joy! They want nothing from it except that you become happy and feel their love, knowing that love of self is the greatest gift one can be given. You will observe this outpouring of devotion in later chapters, as I guide you through my teachings, as written by me in class or following meditation.

It's important to note that a Guide who is channeled does not give specific information about when you will meet the love of your life or when you will join them on the Other Side. As a rule, they don't pinpoint future events and offer nothing about time, as it doesn't exist for them. From their perspective, "time" is just another gift that we humans on the Earth plane use to move through our days, weeks and months.

If you want to meet your own Guides and Angels, you must be prepared to do the work that's necessary to make this happen. And if you choose to embark on that path, I wish for your journey into spirituality to be as pleasurable and satisfying as mine has been.

Chapter Fifteen

It is I, Amadeus

It is I, Amadeus. You learn of me at this time and are amazed by the love that I have for you. The others will surface at a later time.

Loving you, Amadeus.

August of 2007 was an unfathomable turning point in my life. In class, after a guided meditation, I began to write about what I had seen and heard: "Armadeus, wizened old man. 'You are love and light.' White robes. In gazebo. 'I am with you always.'"

Not aware of what this name would come to mean in the future, I spelled it as I heard it. This was my first introduction to a Guide. Imagine my delight when I finally connected with an entity on the Other Side! I had been hearing of this possibility for over a year and found this a blessing of untold joy. I shared the information in class, and my teacher, confirmed this other-worldly introduction, as she was able to see psychically what I saw.

A few months later, as I was writing in my journal one morning after meditation, I heard the words: *"It is I, Armadeus."*

What was that? What did I hear? Was I crazy?

But it came, so I wrote down those exact words. Then "he" went on to say: *"Good morning, Sweet One."*

Still surprised, I continued to write the message, and the words began to flow and pages of rhetoric appeared. That is how it began. Now, glorious, loving messages from the Other Side come to me each time I write with any of my Guides, Angels or Others.

When he first came through, Armadeus always announced his presence with the following words: *"It is I, Armadeus."* (The other Guides and Angels would, in time, develop their own personal introductions, too.) For many months, I wrote with whom I thought was "Armadeus," until one day, out of curiosity, I entered his name in the Google search engine – and discovered Wolfgang Amadeus Mozart. I decided the next morning during meditation to ask for clarity, and so it was given.

"Yes, I was Wolfgang Amadeus Mozart in one of my past lives, and this is the name I am using for you to connect with me. You see, where my spirit energy still exists, we have no need for names to communicate with each other. We are energy souls and take no real form. When I come to you, you need to hear a name to identify which energy is coming to you at any given time. So it is that I have chosen Amadeus, as it is a strong name. And my past lifetime as Wolfgang Amadeus Mozart is chronicled as being extremely gifted with my music and extremely prolific with my voice. It is unto you that I will be unfolding many words of wisdom, as you work with others to heal their pain and their wounds on this Earth plane incarnation of the soul, known this lifetime as Frances.

"You will meet others from the Other Side that are with you also. We are all here to protect you and keep you moving forward. You have many Guides, Angels, Fairies, Gnomes and Others. You will also hear your son one day, when you are so moved to do so. The pain of giving your son back to the Source will continue to lessen with time, and you will not dream of being with him again until it is your turn to cross. That will be your last dream, as you drift out of the Earth body known as Frances and return to the place you came from all of those many years ago.

"Frances, Dear One, you wonder so deeply about so many things that it is difficult for you to slow your mind and allow us to bring messages to you. It is for that very reason that we choose to come quickly into your field, so that you do not become anxious and move on before one of us has

a moment to bring our messages through. So it is that you are a conscious channel, meaning you do remember some of the things that have been said during a channeling session, whereas an unconscious channel does not remember any of the session, as they are deep in meditation, taking quite some time to get there.

"You must trust, trust, trust that you are truly getting the correct messages flowing through your vocal cords and fingers when we come through you. You are willing, and you are wise beyond anything you can comprehend. When our messages come to you and you are in complete faith, you will be unstoppable. We realize that occasionally you are looking for validation of your words, as they come from us through your throat chakra. Sweet One, know that you are deeply and truly loved by us, and you do not need validation. When you are in full trust of that concept, your world will dramatically change once more!"

So it wasn't Armadeus at all – it was Wolfgang *Amadeus* Mozart, the famous composer! As you can see, dear readers, it takes trust and belief that I am a true channel for me to do my chosen work. I now know that I chose it before I came into this lifetime, although I do not remember making this contract. I do not take this task lightly, and I never will. It's a gift that we all may exercise, but many choose not to.

There are so many modalities in the spiritual world. You can become a healer, a channel, a psychic, a medium – the list goes on and on. For example, a healer can send energy to another being, plant, or animal by the laying on of hands, or by setting an intention and sending their energy through the waves of the world's energetic atmosphere. Generally, we choose a few modalities that we feel most comfortable with to study each lifetime and leave the rest for others to explore.

Amadeus is with me to relay sage advice to those who would hear him, as he has lived many times on the Earth plane. He has learned what he was supposed to learn, and no longer incarnates. You will meet many "Others" as I continue my story and share it with you in "*love, light, AND laughter.*" That is his message as he ends each channeling session.

Chapter Sixteen
The Others

It is I, Amadeus. Here is the time in your journey that you learn of the Others. You will love, enjoy and appreciate them with energetic laughter as you move through their introductions.

Loving you, Amadeus.

Justine

And so it is that I have met many of my Guides, Fairies, Angels and Others. The next entity to appear to me, and through me, was Justine, and she arrived through my journaling. Justine is a gentle, motherly soul who comes into the channeling sessions when one of the participants wants to discuss a problem close to their heart and get sage, motherly advice. At those times, Justine hears them and comforts them with her words. She is a loving entity and comes through in my writings when I need mothering, too.

It's so comforting to know the love that surrounds me. I was not aware, until this time in my life, that this love from the Other Side was mine. My strength has always been a given, as I walk this journey, and I have always felt it and lived it; but love of self has been difficult to wrap my arms around. Now, I have finally come to know it, thanks to my unseen friends. It's thrilling to know that if you first love yourself, you are almost flawless in loving others.

Frances Pullin

Mathilda

As I introduce "Mathilda with an 'h,'" I laugh quietly to myself. That is how she came to me one day during writing after meditation, and she was very specific that her name had an 'h' in it! She is a little, dancing Fairy and comes to laugh and play with those who might feel unsettled the first time they sit with me for a channeling session where other entities will be offering advice. She pops in, introduces herself, injects her laughter, and then quickly says *"Ta ta!"* And with that, she is gone! In a session with a group of lovely gals who are mediums, she appeared as a twinkling light to the delight of one of the channels, who was just seeing her first Fairy!

Horatio

I learned during a class meditation the week of November 11, 2007, that Horatio is a Guardian Angel. You will enjoy a session or two with him further on in this section.

Jarod

One of my Angels that I have met is Jarod, and I say "met'" tongue in cheek! Many years ago, on an ordinary day, as I was taking my younger sons to school, I found myself asking them for help to stay calm so that "no one would be hurt." An accident seemed to be in my energy field. I did not know where or when – I just knew it was to be. I asked my Angels for help, too.

Oh, how I did not like the traffic around the junior high school! I always became a bit agitated as it backed up and I'd watch the moms making sure their children got safely onto the school grounds. I wondered why most cars did not pull all the way to the end of the driveway so that others could also drop off their children. The practical side of me is often present, as I see the whole picture – not just the little one I am in at the moment; and I do tend to get less agitated about the small stuff these days, as I learn not to judge others and embrace my spirituality. This newfound calm is yet another blessing that has come from loving myself.

It is I, Amadeus

But on this particular day that's become etched in my very soul, I felt apprehensive. I dropped the boys off at their school, then forced myself to calmly drive to a client's home in Huntington Beach – an area I'm not familiar with – to install some designer pillows and chair cushions. I finished my task and left, but as I proceeded out the gate of this community, I witnessed the cleanup of a car accident in the intersection I was approaching.

Glass and debris were everywhere. The police were also everywhere, and I could not turn in the direction I needed to go. I pulled up to a police officer in the intersection who appeared to be directing traffic. He was a handsome young man, and when our eyes connected, I felt an outpouring of warmth and love. (Trust me, I knew he was years younger in his physical body than me, but I couldn't help smiling inside and feeling beautiful.) We smiled at each other, and I asked for directions. He gave them to me, and I followed his instructions, turning left exactly as he had directed.

Suddenly, there was the sound of screeching brakes, and in that instant I saw I was about to collide with my client, who was just returning home, if I didn't quickly turn the wheel. BAM! I had mistakenly been guided to pull into oncoming traffic and was hit by a great big, brand new, red Suburban! You'd think I would have seen that much red blazing toward me, but somehow I didn't. Now, in the midst of the accident scene, with glass in my mouth, I looked for my handsome police officer to come help me.

My eyes scanned the group of officers, but he was nowhere in sight. How could that be? He was just there! Why did he not want to come and help me? In a few minutes, another officer came to the car to check on me. We waited together for the firemen to open the door and assure everyone that I was OK. I asked for water to clear my mouth, but alas, there was none, so I just smiled, as I was in shock but not acknowledging it. Remember, I am strong and independent!

The car was completely totaled, but fortunately, I had hurt no one! The blow from the red suburban (not my client's car – she had avoided the crash) had spun me 180 degrees and taken off the back right wheel.

It's the side where my youngest son always sat, and it was completely destroyed. Had he been in that seat, buckled up, there would not have been much protection for him. That's when I knew for sure that my Guardian Angel had been with me! He had heard my plea. He'd helped me stay safe through the accident energy I'd been feeling and to not hurt anyone else – the fear I'd voiced to my sons; then he had disappeared.

There have been several car accidents in my lifetime that were life-threatening, but I always came through without a scratch. This was just another one, but I realized that this time I'd actually seen and met the Guardian Angel who'd kept me safe through all of them. And he had filled my heart with joy.

A few weeks later, following meditation, I began to write and the name Jarod came into my mind. I laughed out loud and wrote, "You are my Angel, and you were at the accident! I know you! I love you!" He then admitted that yes, it was he who'd been with me each time I'd needed him. Then I began to understand the outpouring of love from that policeman that day! He was not an ordinary policeman, but an Angel who loved me and saved me.

You may wonder why I love Jarod, even though, in human form as a policeman, he had directed me into oncoming traffic! After all, things could have turned out quite differently – I could have been seriously hurt or have injured someone else. But I began to realize that Jarod had picked the red Suburban – and not my client's small Cadillac – so that the driver was protected by the size of his vehicle. He'd also picked where I'd been positioned during the accident. The back passenger side of the car had caved in, not the driver's side. Now, when I'm in my car and feeling overwhelmed with traffic, or when someone else is driving their car and I'm being a "backseat driver," questioning their driving, I just bring Jarod to mind to calm me, and to be reminded that I am safe and still have many long years on this Earth.

Nostradamus

The next guide I met and worked with – and am excited to tell you about – is Nostradamus. I know that sounds quite bold, but it was *very* exciting when he came through in my writings. He is the boldest of the guides whom I have met thus far. His voice is booming at times when I channel him, but he's very loving and his advice is always "spot on," as is the advice of the others. The client I was channeling for when Nostradamus decided to come through and speak asked if this entity was the same Nostradamus who had walked the Earth plane and made such startling predictions. Nostradamus stated that he was indeed the same soul energy, but he was no longer coming back into the Earth plane. He was here to give advice, not to make predictions. And so it is that Nostradamus comes through when he is needed, and his advice is always sage, wise and loving.

To clarify: I offer channeling sessions to others so that they may have their questions answered with prudent advice. I never reveal what goes on during a session, keeping strict confidentiality to protect each person's privacy. Some clients ask extremely personal questions, and, thank goodness, I forget most of what they asked and were told. A client may record the session, if they wish. At times, I have found that the recording remains blank, as the Guides did not want to have the information recorded; they just wanted it to be remembered. Their powerful energy can make this happen.

Mother Theresa

As I mentioned above, another guide I've met is called Mother Theresa. Yes, she has crossed into Spirit, but is continuing the work she did on Earth during her final incarnation. She is my healing Guide, and I'm pleased and honored that she's working through me. In fact, I'd like to share a story about her work with a young man called Erich who'd developed a facial "tick" that was driving him insane. He'd had it for six months by the time he called me seeking advice, and I promised I'd do some work and get back to him.

Later that week, while meditating, I brought a question forward about Erich and what he could do to heal himself. A loving, soft-spoken woman came into my writing, introduced herself as Mother Theresa, and gave me words to say to him. I sent those exact words to Erich by e-mail, and he was very grateful. I know he has healed, as he sent me a huge "Thank you!"

Apostle Paul

I have had other Guides and Angels come through, but I do not channel them vocally. I only write with them when they have something they would like to tell me about what's going on in my life at that particular time. Those who I only write with appear seldom and do not need a voice for their messages, as they are meant for me alone or to pass on to a client for healing. I would be pleased to meet more of these entities, in writing or in channeling. Should that happen, I will be happy to share them with all of you!

Chapter Seventeen

Sharing Private Notes

It is I, Amadeus. As you share the most private notes from your journaling with all of your audience, you will be allowing others to judge you. You ask that they not judge, but unless they are truly on their spiritual path, they will judge. May you move forward in confidence that your soul is up to this judgment and will forever love you.

Amadeus.

It is at this time that I will share some very private notes. The information will be revealed to you, as it was to me. There are Others dictating to me, and so I am just the vessel, receiving these words and writing them in my most private journals. The journals began in 2007, and I continue them to this day. I enjoy re-reading them, as they bring such pleasure as I review my spiritual growth through the teachings. It's clear that I have been led into my destiny.

When I first began journaling, I was so thrilled each time I wrote that I would want to share it with others in my circle of friends. Imagine their boredom! First and foremost, they were not spiritually-minded (and may never be), and here was this grown woman with grown children and grandchildren acting like a love-struck teen! She was talking about loving herself... How preposterous was that? Well, it's true! I do love each and every one of my Guides and Others, and most of all myself! Coming to that realization has been a long road, but I made it. And you can, too!

In the beginning, there was no need for any of my Guides to identify themselves with a unique introduction, as there were only a couple of them, but that changed as more and more came on board. As time progressed, it was clear that the opportunity to chat with me became an honor for them, and they began to introduce themselves with individual flair. (You'll see their unique introductions as you read on.)

In this chapter and those that follow, you'll witness me asking a question and see how an entity comes forward to give me an answer. Whether I'm writing or channeling their words, I do not correct what they say. The entities do not actually "speak" on the Other Side; they communicate telepathically through me, and their words can be clumsy or eloquent. Sometimes a word is misplaced or misspoken, as they have not used verbal language since they transitioned the last time. They need to speak to me so that I can communicate their messages, and what you'll read in this book is the actual verbiage from my journals.

Typically, I ask a question before meditation and am answered by the appropriate entity. These friends from the Other Side seem to sense who is needed in a reading, and I always have my journal handy with the current date at the top of the page. These journals have chronicled my journey. If you are comfortable with this method, then you might want to try it, too.

When you write with your Guides, date each page. If you receive a message you want to be private, simply tear it out and throw it away, or put it in a safe place. Over the years, I've only discarded one or two, so it's unlikely that you'll be inundated with tough teachings! Still, you want to protect your privacy and feel safe, and you never know when your journal will be picked up by another person and your secret messages exposed. That's why I throw away information I don't want other eyes to see. I don't feel that *all* my communications are for public consumption! Therefore, the only things you'll read here are those that I feel comfortable divulging. After all, one day, I, too, will pass from this earth, and my private messages will remain private. No Hollywood novels about me!

Before I share some of my private notes, I want to say that trust is a tremendous sensation when it is gained. All that I teach you begins with trust. In the beginning of my journey, I received messages from many entities on the Other Side. That slowed over the years. I understand that when their message has been delivered, and they are sure it has been heard, they move on to teach other souls on the Earth plane about love. Never are they gone completely, as I am still able to call on any one of them for specific information if I know which Guide or Angel I need at a given time.

As I've mentioned before, my primary Guide is Amadeus, and most answers come from him. And so we begin...

Why am I here? (11-15-07)

"It is I, Amadeus. You are to go forward and heal others and release their pain. The way will be shown to you in the coming weeks and months. You must clear yourself of the pain of yesteryear and make way for the joy that is to become yours. You must find the joy before you are able to move in a direction becoming to you. What say, what direction? (Keep in mind, as I mentioned earlier, that they sometimes use words and expressions unlike those you and I use.) *We will show you, and you will know it to be true. When you have profound questions, you will ask for us to answer. You must trust that we are love and you will be safe with us.*

"Go now; fill your heart with amazing love and light. That is what we ask of you this night. Use your skills to help yourself, and others will learn from your example. We are with you, and you will leave with love in your heart, knowing we have filled it with love. That is our gift to you. Love yourself and heal all pain. Amadeus."

How long have you been with me? (11-20-07)

"We have spent untold lifetimes with you and will be with you always."

Frances Pullin

Where do you come from?

"We come from the Universe, and we know you need us to be with you on your eternal journey.

**What about Colleen
(a friend who had recently crossed into the Light)?**

"You have talked about her before. She wishes to convey that she is happy. Relay this message to her children in any way that you can." (Tim Braun, the medium I worked with after my son's passing, had also spoken of Colleen.)

How can I relieve my sorrow over Damon?

"You need to smile when you think of him and let it go, as he is happy and at peace. You must remember you are in charge of his daughter and she needs to see you being strong. You need to remove the symbols in the home and let other family members grieve in their own way." (One of these "symbols" was the cookie jar I'd given Damon when his daughter was born, and it still remains tucked in the corner of my kitchen counter. This cookie jar, dubbed "Big Bird," would not take it lightly if it was shoved into a cupboard! Someday, it will rest in Morgan's kitchen, as there are many cookie stories packed into it.)

**Who is sending this message,
and what other message do you have for me?**

"This is Horatio. We want you to go forth and continue on this path and teach others about this work being done. Just continue to be patient, loving and giving. A plan is in place to bring you back into the living, and along with it there will be many rewards. Continue to make contact with us. You will see a pattern that leads you where you need to go."

Am I ready to read for others?

"Yes, you are ready. Go forth and enlighten those who seek you. Do not let them use it as a tool to go forward with their lives with too many sessions. They, too, must do the work you are doing."

And so, dear friends, when you are ready, you will do the work it takes to communicate with the Other Side. Hopefully, you will be as thankful and grateful as I am.

As we move forward through the messages I received over the years, you will see the personality of each Guide or Angel unfold. If you have questions or need guidance as you read further, I will be ready to assist through my website, www.Angels-Healing-Hearts.com. I will answer any questions you have about the content of this book. Should you wish to receive information from any of my Guides, there will be a place for you to call, set an appointment, and pay for such assistance from them. English is my only language, so please keep that in mind. Should there be a need for translation, I will deal with it as it arises. Know that I care for each of you and will do my best to be there for you. There are many of us in the spiritual community who are happy and willing to assist you on your journey.

The most important thing to know, when seeking a teacher, is to ask your Angels and Guides if you have found the right person. Go with instinct. If you feel you are being used or have outgrown a teacher, move on. Don't let your head get in the way. Instinct is found in the heart and comes from the Others who surround you. Listen to it. The Others have much to tell, so listen and act upon what you hear. To this day, I find little things in a mess when I don't pay attention to what is being told to me in my ear or my heart. For example, I might hear, *"Don't forget the book!"* on my way out the door, but don't listen. Then, when I arrive at my destination without it, I'm disappointed in myself. Listen, listen, listen, and then follow what you hear.

Frances Pullin

Do you have a message for me? (11-28-07)

"You are worried. Do not fear. We are watching over you and, too, your situation. Stress not. Go forward again."

Why have I found you? Will I know you in my next body?

"You know us now because you seek to know. Each lifetime has its own trials. You will only know we are with you if you listen for us, as you learned in this lifetime."

Who is here today?

"Amadeus, Horatio, Jarod, Mathilda, Kristen, and Kendra are with you."

Is there another message?

"Go forth and be not afraid, as we stand beside you. Teach of what you have learned through these writings and other seekers may know of the existence of their Guides and Angels."

What can you tell me today about another life I have lived?

"You were just a young thing and delighted all who knew you, but illness took you before your time and that is why you think positive thoughts about your state of health and ability to handle all disease. You must ask for help from us and recognize you are not alone. God is here in all of us and in you. Ask and you will receive."

Is there anything else before we leave tonight?

"We are bringing gifts of joy, and you will know they are from us. Look for them. We love you. Goodbye until we share with you again."

It is I, Amadeus

What is your message this day? (12-6-07)

"You are the love of Source. Go forth with this knowledge and trust that you see what others may not. Teach of love, letting negativity go and allow judgment to disappear. You will rise to great heights when you come to trust completely that you are one with this process. Want not, as we will clothe and feed you. Your journey is filled with many riches and you will be able once again to gift those less fortunate than you. The gifts will be of love and money. You have been sharing your wealth and gifts throughout this lifetime and lifetimes before this! Know you will be fine and know that your miracle is near at hand. Trust in us, trust the Source, and trust in Frances. Go in peace, knowing we are at work with and for you. Love from us forever."

As I write this, I want to make sure you understand my doubts about sharing my journey. In the beginning of this process, I was thrilled, frightened, and questioning when receiving messages from the Other Side. Was I just a fool for believing all I was being told?

Some days I pleaded from the depths of my soul for a sign that I was on my true path, and, over and over again, I would feel that I was awakening to what I had known throughout this entire lifetime. It took the return of my son Damon to the Source to catapult me forward. I was told by those who wrote with me that it was he who had set me in motion in order to understand that he's safe and happy. I see him smiling as I write this now. He sits on my right shoulder, and sometimes he whispers in my ear. He is thrilled, as are the Others with him, that I am sitting at my desk this morning, devoting time to giving you the gifts that you need. Whether you're already practicing spirituality, or just beginning to enter the realm, you may need a lift at times, and it is with love and light and laughter that I give that gift to you!

Chapter Eighteen

Healing

It is I, Amadeus. Greetings, Sweet One. You are beginning to heal from your loss of your son, known as Damon. It is a difficult journey and the healing may never be complete. Alas, as you go forward you will experience times of great joy within the family and times of sadness. Do not falter. It is your journey and will be your journey without judgment.

Love, Amadeus.

I ask Amadeus to tell me about himself. (1-31-08)

"Yes, many years ago, I, too, walked the Earth. I was also reborn, but have lived successfully and learned my lessons. Thus, many years ago, I became entangled with your spirit and have remained since. You, too, are learning, and one day you will cease to incarnate, but for now it is our job to guide you. I am a Guide. I teach you how to live productively. I am unlike an Angel, who protects you from great harm. I walk just with you. You are a handful! Your spirit is very energetic and filled with mirth. You do not smile as much this lifetime, as you have handled a great sadness, but you are coming back to life and laughter."

Mathilda joins us this same morning. She is giving advice as I ponder a new place of employment.

"Mathilda says to relax. You are beginning a new leg of your journey, oh Sweet One. Do not falter. Trust in us and trust in Frances. You know which job is the right one. Your patience will take you there. You will learn faith and trust, hope and prayer. Sweet One, you have jumped over many bushes and darted through the forest, and are coming out on the sunny side! Go forth and dance!"

As you may remember, Mathilda is a fairy, and this is how she teases me about being more playful and carefree.

During a channeling class on 2-7-08, I wrote: "Michelle (my daughter) is going to Afghanistan. She is treating it as an adventure." In turn, I heard the following:

"No, she knows how serious this is. She is trained and in training. She pretends so one does not know her true feelings. She is surrounded by Angels and will be safe. She is a warrior, no a warrior-ess. She understands your love and worry and is making sure you and she will be together for your sake, not hers. Go in peace, knowing she is safe and will return."

No one came forth to claim the above session, so maybe it was in unison that they sent the message.

At the age of 34, my daughter decided to join the Air Force Reserves. Michelle desperately wanted to become a helicopter pilot, and she felt this was her chance. Unfortunately, she was too old to be a pilot, but she joined the Air Force anyway. This adventurous woman became a helicopter repair person, knowing that riding in these "birds" was as close as she would get to flying one. So, after basic training, she was assigned to Davis Monthon Air Force Base in Tucson, Arizona.

With others in her group of Reservists, she flew to Afghanistan in early 2009 to fight to protect the freedom of the United States of America. When disabled helicopters needed repair, she was called from the safety of the base and into the field to repair them. She never told me when she left the camp and went out in danger, but I would know she was gone because she would not be on Facebook for days. Because I am a psychic, and her mother, I knew in my heart that she was out of the safe arms of the base, and I prayed for her safety.

Michelle is proud of her decision to join the Reserves, and it has made her confident, outgoing, and bold. She's no longer the shy, little one she used to be, and her desire for travel has been realized. Today, she takes frequent business trips, and her Air Force duties take her all over the country and sometimes for weeks to foreign lands. She had always traveled in her mind through books, and now she travels in real life. It's wonderful, as a mother, to see this new persona unfold before my eyes.

I am proud of my daughter's decision to defend her country. She is in a place where she has been in many lifetimes – protecting her countrymen. According to my Guides, Michelle has been a soldier many times. She is walking in her Light and has joined me on many retreats, as we walk the familiar path of lives before this one and continue our spiritual journey together. And my courageous daughter loves to be in California for the Holistic Faires at the School of Multidimensional Healing Arts and Sciences!

What do I need to heal now?
What needs to be resolved and why? (2-13-08)

"You need to resolve your jealousy of those you know who fare better than you and do not have to join the workforce. This work is for your personal growth and enlightenment. You are a creative one, and you are wasting away in the chair and at the computer screen. Go forth in life and remember that you need to know how to take care of Frances at all times. You have taken care of you by yourself and will do so again someday.

"You need to be learning and advancing your mind and glowing in your praises. Go forth and take the bite out of your communications. You are putting yourself on a pedestal, and it is not pretty. As your Guide, Amadeus, I am giving you firm advice. Do not falter in it. You are hurting those who love you. If they are sharp-tongued, then smile and bless them and their day. Wish them well, and all goodness will return to you and yours. You will find immeasurable wealth and happiness as you have never known before.

"Go forth, Sweet One, and enjoy what I have taught you this night. Go in peace. We love you and you need to remember to love you!"

I want to remind you that these messages from the Others presented here are not about the person I am today. At that time, I had much growth at hand, and I'm sharing these personal messages with you as an example of their teachings. Back then, I *did* have jealousy and judgment of others, but I have worked very hard to leave that behind and to practice what they have taught me.

I would like you to feel the love that is present as the Others begin to take me further into the unfolding newness that is me. It is the truest blessing to know that there are those on the Other Side so lovingly ready to teach what they have learned before reaching the point of no longer returning to Earth, and to guide those of us still here through our tribulations. That is part of my message to you. Learn what I have learned through my teachers, and listen to yours when you resolve to become the best *you* that you can be in this lifetime. Love yourself and instill love of self in your children. There have been many messages saying to love yourself first and love of others will follow. I do hope that you understand the love with which I am being guided. No attempt to embarrass is ever used as a teaching tool by those on the Other Side, and never any sarcasm. Just firm advice for the protection of my soul.

Chapter Nineteen

Learning Trust

It is I, Amadeus. Trust, trust, trust, trust, trust. That is my message for this day.

Love and light, Amadeus.

What are you teaching me tonight? (2-17-08)

"The secret you are looking for is to be revealed to you this night. You are asking this so healing can take place. I am here to inform you that, through many reincarnates, you have been a spiritual leader. You have spoken of love of God. This is why you do not covet the building that others stand inside. You know the stories to be interpreted according to the storyteller. You know God's truth and you will once again go forth with trust for those who will listen. Trust yourself with the wonder of this gift. You have other lessons to learn and past hurts to heal, but this has never been one of them. Go forth and shout with joy! I am Sara, an Angel who walks with you on these journeys. I love you and love that you love and teach God's truths. Trust, trust, trust. You are safe. You have not been in harm's way. You have been protected by all of us at any given time during this incarnation. We are working with you on this as we have done throughout your journey of knowing us. You will gain trust with each smile you smile *and each tear you shed. Go forth in trust and security that you are safe, Sweet One!"*

My initial reaction, many years ago at that dinner at my parents' home – and a fear now gaining momentum with my newfound spirituality – was fear of Source. This fear had its roots in the religion I'd been taught as a child – so different from the spirituality I'd been learning since 2007. I was living in truth now, with a new set of beliefs from the ones I'd held as a child and young woman. Source (or what many call God) had always been a part of my life, but now I was learning not to fear It/Him/Her, as Source is an all-encompassing love. I was learning to trust that I was finally on the right path, and that evil was not lurking in the shadows waiting to hijack my sad and listless soul. I was in control now. Me! Once afraid of everything – staying in the "box," so to speak – I now had a voice. You, too, are being taught by that voice! You are now awakening to your highest potential, just as I have done! I had to trust, as I trust you to do, that I was questioning everything that was being shown to me and that, consequently, I was coming out of the darkness and into the light. My belief in what I was being shown became the strongest friend I had as I emerged into my truth, and I realized that it was Damon's crossing that had nudged me forward on this journey.

As you may now be aware, my Guides use the word "God" frequently as they teach me my lessons, but I have chosen to use "Source" in this book when not quoting them. There are many words for this Higher Power, and I don't judge those who use different terms or have spiritual or religious beliefs other than mine. I am using "Source" to show you that there are many words for this Energy, and all are correct. We must all use the term we are most comfortable with.

I have learned over time that not all who wish to be spiritual *are* spiritual. It is for this reason that you will often hear me say, "Question, question, and question!" I want you to question everything I tell you and that others tell you until it resonates with you; until your intuition tells you that you have found your light.

There will be things in this book you agree with, and things that you disagree with. Take what makes your heart swell with happiness and question the rest. There are many books on this subject written at many different levels, and when you find a passage in this book that you questioned before but now find it written in a way that's clear to you, then and only then do you own it.

Sit with your personal Guides and Others. Meditate. Write with these entities and trust what you are being taught. By knowing for sure that you believe a concept presented in these pages, you'll be more able to live in that belief and knowledge, as it is substantiated by your Divine Guidance.

What is your message today? (3-10-08)

During a telephone conversation in early March 2009, I was about to say something a little sarcastic about how someone was making decisions about financial business and their life path, and I'd caught myself in judgment and jealousy. Then I remembered the message received on February 13th from Amadeus and realized that to not judge is difficult, but not impossible. I'd also learned that jealousy is unbecoming, and to be happy with what I have chosen my life to be. So as you can see, I am learning to be less judgmental, and I ask that you, too, stop judging others and their behavior. I have chosen, during my times on the Other Side, to be a hard worker, and I have continued on that path each day here on Earth.

"It is I, Amadeus. You are strong and sure. You have done the right thing with your phone caller and caught yourself doing so. Good job, Sweet One. Be proud and filled with love of self and others. You have grown and are growing still in love of self. It is a wonderful thing to do. We will all be here to help with your healing. Visit often, as we love being one with you. All things have their season and this is your season of love and growth. Trust that your employment is nearing and you will kick yourself for not enjoying all of your days and not getting your house in order. Trust Kevin that he will know the right things to add to your prosperity, Sweet One. Love him and continue to enjoy your days with him. Now go quietly and fill your day. Love, Amadeus."

My Guides and Others have been teaching me and loving me for my entire lifetime. I always move forward, stubbing my toe occasionally by reaching for judgment, and often have to get out of my own way. I've found that when I put judgment aside, I live life in a more gentle and loving way. You, too, can reach for a more blessed feeling on this Earth plane – just move gently with yourself as you travel this journey. First and foremost, do not judge you. Love you. Each day that ends, is over. We can't return to it to change it. Accept that concept, and don't dwell on what was and what can't be changed. The only thing that can be changed is a gentler tomorrow. It's up to you!

The next message came through during a time when I'd been laid off. It's difficult to be in this position and not feel disrespected. Being part of the cut was absolutely no reflection on me, but my ego had been wounded. It took many lessons like the one above to get me back out there and into the workforce. The building industry was suffering, and my job had been designing upgrades for new homes being purchased. As the builder I worked for began to crumble, so did my position. Then, after an outstanding introduction to an innovative company, I landed a fabulous new job!

I went forward with calmness and confidence, thanks to my team on the Other Side and their continued loving messages. I'd love to tell you I was still with that great company, but the tumble of the housing industry continued and soon I was again without work and with no desire to continue to work the long hours of that industry. Even in an almost perfect environment, the work was taxing. I found myself making great money, but with great loss of time with my family. Days began at 7 a.m. and sometimes ended at one in the morning. My self-respect finally outgrew the desire for a big pay check, and I put in fewer hours, earned fewer dollars, and ultimately the showroom closed. The industry had been good to me, but my days with it were over.

Sometimes the simplest thing, such as loving yourself, removes you from the oversized paychecks and the stress of long work days. No longer sporting a bruised ego, I accepted my unemployment checks and the even pace of my new day! But boredom soon set in and I rewrote my resume for a less taxing position, culminating in a volunteer position with SMHAS, where no resume was required.

**I know you have words for me this day!
Do let me know your guidance. (5-7-08)**

"It is I, Amadeus. Hello. You are to see you. You are to love you. The calm surrounding you is amazing. Go now and pick up the phone, make a call, finish your application. The interviewing will begin anew, but you are now ready and able to move forward. Look at you. You are a professional. You will knock them dead and you will work because you want to, not because you need to! It will take the longevity from your days and your home chores will become more pressing, thus getting done. There is no magic in your mirror, only the reflection of a much-loved, self-assured woman whose time has come. It is time for her to shine her light, impress the boss, and accept the career until it is no longer necessary for Frances to do so. Go, Sweet One, enjoy the day!"

Chapter Twenty

Following the Path

It is I, Amadeus. Sweet One, you have decided to continue your path in spirituality. We stand proud of you. Go forward and reap the rewards.

Love to you, Amadeus.

By 2008, I was well into my spiritual journey, continuing to follow the path I'd been shown and explore it more fully. It was a year of changes, and I dialogued often in meditation and writing with my friends on the Other Side This became a good time for me to follow the path I had begun, explore it more fully, and continue my meditation and self-help practices.

How does anger serve me? (6-10-08)

"Anger does not serve you well. There has been too much of it in your lifetimes. It is time to heal and go with love. Love of family, love of husband, love of children and love of life. You must let go of any sharp tongue as it will hurt those around you. Love as God loves you. Speak of God's love for all you meet. Accept love back into your heart and mind. Dust off your heart and fill it only with love and tolerance. Therefore, Sweet One, go forth and prepare God's blessings for all. We will help, but you must hear yourself and stop in your tracks."

My husband had retired and was sitting on the sofa most of the day. As I joined him there, staring out the living room window, I grew weary of the nothingness and would snap at his comments, even though he was only chatting. But Kevin saw through my anxiety and continued to talk with me with all-embracing patience. He loves me to a depth I have not known in this lifetime.

I was waiting for something to happen to raise me from that sofa, but did not know what it would be. What I did know was that it was through my own misery that I was creating an unhappy environment for both of us. I'm proud that at least I knew I needed help, and so I asked Spirit for direction. Again, my Guides and Angels loved me enough to tell me how to move forward. I took their advice and began more meditation, teaching me that time is precious and should be treated as such. A short time later, my husband and I began to study real estate, got our licenses, and started working together.

I continue to study spirituality and can't seem to get enough, as I'm always eager for more information and proof that what I'm studying is true. The best confirmation, of course, is writing with the Others, because they confirm what I'm learning.

As I am writing this day, I feel anxious again. Sara, your name came to me. Is it you who are with me? (7-1-08)

"Yes, Sweet One, it is Sara. You are anxious today, but not like last time when Amadeus assisted. This is about money, for you and for Devin. You turned down a job you feel might have saved you. It would've made you ill. There were too many hours, demeaning instruction, and no family love and life. Devin will be at work soon and you will know your job has been successful. You worry now that you have upset Michelle. She is fine, but having trouble with her new schedule. Your dear friend, Vickie, put it so well: Once you have thanked Source, thank yourself for being such a wonderful, thoughtful woman. You are dear to many. Love Frances as Source would have you do. Now, calm yourself. Take a deep breath and hug you! You, Sweet One, can slay the dragon! Love, Sara."

And then I heard:

"Play, girlfriend! Go out and laugh! Do not be so serious. See the birds in their nest. They are ready to fly, and so should you! Remember we all love you and want happiness. Go then. Play away the day! Map out a route and then ignore it! Do what pleases you and you alone. Then, laugh over dinner and keep a light burning for those yet to come. Play, Sweet One! With love, Mathilda."

And finally:

"Good morning, Frances. It is I, Amadeus. You know we all love you. ("All" means all my Guides, Angels, Fairies, and Others who watch over me from the Other Side, including Damon and my parents.) *Be settled and have a play day. Goodbye."*

Chapter Twenty One
Meditation Choices

Ah, it is I, Amadeus. Your Guided Meditations take your students into loving places where they find the peace and tranquility they are seeking. They are so gentle, and the sound of your voice soothes the soul from their drive in the traffic to attend your classes. You are guiding them through relaxation, chakra clearing, and into a sacred space where they are invited to meet one of their Guides or Others. It is here that you bring such peace to so many and lift them up on their journeys. We thank you for this time.

Love, Amadeus.

And so, dear reader, you are seeing that there is nothing but love and laughter from my Guides and Angels for me. Your "Others" feel that for you, as well. Some of you already know of this love and laughter, but alas, many of you don't. If I do nothing more with this book than get just one of you to begin your journey into spirituality and learn love of self, then it's been worth every minute! Know that it all begins with love of self.

Self-love is something all of us need to bring into our hearts. It can be a daunting task, but once mastered it brings unadulterated joy! To do this, go into your heart space, stand in front of a mirror and look deeply into your eyes. Say "I love you" and use your first name. Do this as often as possible until you come to peace with loving you.

This is a practice to teach your children. We all tell our children we love them, and they reply that they love us too. But does your child know who the perfect he/she is? They are born perfect. They may be tall or short, plump or thin, quick to laugh or throw a tantrum. They are still perfect and should be allowed to love themselves. It is life's greatest gift. If all of us loved each other, wars would end and peace could come to the Earth. Let that resonate, and then read on.

In the next few paragraphs, I give you a short guided meditation. After you've read it, put the book down and try it. By "guided," I mean that I guide you with my words, but as you do it, you'll go where your mind wants to wander. There are no rules, only the vibration of love.

Sit quietly and think of nothing but your breath. Just breathe in slowly and breathe out slowly three times, holding your breath before breathing out. I will now lead you through the meditation...

Relax. Relax completely. Unfurl your brow and release the tension there. Move to your cheeks, eyes and jaws. Release their tension also. Move to your shoulders, neck, arms and hands. Wiggle you fingers and relax even more. Now relax your torso, hips, legs and toes. Find yourself at peace with you.

Picture the flat, round red chakra at the body's root. (If you don't see anything, just imagine it. This is not meant to be a weary practice, but one filled with imagination and joy.) Fill the root chakra with white light and see it open and spinning.

Now do this with the bright orange chakra at your sacral space, and again with the yellow chakra at your solar-plexus. Moving further up the body, unlock the heart chakra, the color of emerald green. Fill it with white light, and you will see the chakra spin faster. Next, move to the throat and envision the cobalt blue of this chakra. Clear it with the white light and see it spin.

Next, move to the throat and envision the cobalt blue of this chakra, clear it and see it spin. Now on to the third eye chakra between the eyebrows, which is a vivid purple. Clear it too and see it spin. The last chakra to open is the crown chakra. Here you will find white light entering the chakra from above the head. It may mix with the purple of the third eye chakra below to become soft lavender, or it may remain white.

Now we are going to do a relaxing visualization. Find yourself at the edge of the ocean and picture what you see there. Are there birds, dolphins or mermaids? What smells are tickling your nose with their distinct flavors? Walk in the sand and observe the cliff above you. You are being guided to slowly move toward the cliff. Again, what do you see, hear and smell? Notice it all.

Walk along the cliff until you arrive at a forest. Step into the forest. Are there pine trees, birch trees, or aspen? As you meander down the path through your personal forest, you will come to a meadow. You are observing untold beauty! Perhaps there is a babbling brook with a log to sit upon. You hear the meadow come alive with crickets, birds and squirrels playing a game of chase. As you sit down on the log, you see a figure coming toward you. Observe the clothing worn by this visitor. Is it a man or a woman? What type of shoes is he/she wearing? Invite them to sit with you. They will chat and possibly give you a name and tell you what they represent, be it Angel, Fairy, or Guide.

This beautiful being has a message and/or a gift for you. Hold out your hand if you are receiving a gift and listen quietly for a message. (This is quite personal. You may choose to share with others what you heard and received, or you may just write it down.) Thank your friend and receive a warm embrace.

Now, stand and wave goodbye. Retrace your steps and leave the meadow, the forest and the cliff. When you are back at the water's edge, sit quietly once more. Breathe deeply, and when you feel ready, softly open your eyes. (I am including a guided meditation on my website as a free download. Visit <u>angels-healing-hearts.com</u>.)

Bring forth the messages you have for me this day. (7-8-08)

"The message we have for you this day continues to be about you having trust in all of us. Trust that God has sent you on this path so that you

might learn trust as you have never known it! It comes from Love. Love from us, love from God, and love from family and friends. Kevin loves you with profound adoration. He trusts you to love him. You must have blind trust that he will handle this issue at hand. (I have no recollection of what "this issue" was, but remembered to trust Kevin, as I have always done.) *You have trusted him always, but he will do it in his time, not yours. Trust him, trust God, trust the Universe, and trust us. We have proven to you we are really there with you at all times on this journey, and on many others. Thank you for finding us and trusting our messages. Go forth in Love and Trust. Amen."*

So, you see, I'm to trust my husband, Kevin, as much as I trust the Universe. Kevin has been put on my path during this current journey on the Earth plane. In counsel, before birth, we agreed to live out our lives with each other for support. We've had a couple of bumps on this path, but so small they have been forgotten. We lean on each other when times are difficult and laugh together when times are happy. We have forged through our grieving of Damon in our own ways, and neither forgets to remember him to the other as thoughts and memories surface. Since we withstood that time together, we know we can withstand anything.

We always enjoy much laughter with family and friends and find that birthday gatherings have moved from restaurants into our home. I have a reputation for picking a recipe, perusing its ingredients, combining them artfully, and cooking up dishes that inspire celebration with each bite. From soups to odd vegetable dishes, from appetizers to the occasional desert, people enjoy being at my table. With it comes laughter and memories to delight each of us. When family comes from out of town, they don't expect to eat out. They want to laugh with us in our kitchen or dining room and make another memory of us together in our new home. Friends find friendship at our table.

Go now and make your new memories.

On a sun-drenched summer day, June 7, 2008, Kevin II married his forever girlfriend, Amy, in a beautiful ceremony attended by many friends and family. We have known Amy and her family for many years and blessed their union. Though I didn't fully realize it then, I was having some trouble knowing that Kevin II, now 26, would not be living at home anymore. He hadn't moved out during his college years, since he'd attended a local school in Irvine – in fact, his college and employment had always been within driving distance of home. What better way to save money than to live at home with us!

Along with Kevin II's marriage came some household changes. We'd moved Michelle's son, Devin, into our home when she'd left for Afghanistan. Now, with Kevin II gone, we rearranged his room for Devin. (Sean, our youngest son, had been living in a bachelor pad, so he was already on his own.) During all these changes, I was having anxiety, but I could not place the source.

Since my Guides are with me always, they know me better than I know myself. They have the innate ability to know the future and the present, and I don't. At first, I thought the anxiety I was feeling was related to Michelle in Afghanistan, but knew instinctively that she would come home safely. So what was it from? Devin? We had him with us for the summer and loved him dearly, so his time with us would be fun. No, that was not it. So imagine my surprise upon finding out, through journal writing with my Guides, that I was deeply missing another of my boys, Kevin II. Although not taken and given back to the Source, like Damon, he had been taken away nonetheless.

I am feeling anxious in life. What do you have to tell me? (7-18-08)

"It is I, Amadeus. You have come to the right place, Dear One. When you are feeling anxious, you will know that you have forgotten you have given yourself to the Universal Source. Keep that in mind and know the days are shaping up the way they are meant to. Devin has filled Kevin II's room, but has not filled his place in your heart. You have him so that Michelle is less burdened by his responsibility. You are seeing Afghanistan in the news. You have been told you will see her again and she will make changes in herself, but she will be safe. Fear not, Dear One. Your plate is full. You have not lost Kevin II, but given him unto Amy to continue his growth along his path on his personal journey. Rest your mind, sleep a

deep sleep, and write down your dreams, as they have much to say. Good night, Sweet One. You are loved."

Sean had moved out the first year and a half of college. He'd moved back home to heal after his brother's crossing, and then he moved out again. It seemed normal to have him come and go. But, it wasn't normal for Kevin to live elsewhere and indeed he would be living with Amy. I heeded my Guides' advice, rested my mind, slept a deep sleep, wrote down my dreams and came to a place of quiet. No longer did I hold the anxiety that I would experience another great loss with Kevin's departure from our home I had just had a sweet, life-changing moment watching, as Amy and her family joined ours and I was now fully realizing the magnificence of it all.

The following type of writing does not happen often. In fact, I had forgotten it happened at all. There was no written question from me to solicit this information, but during this time, my son Sean was holding me up as we readied our home for sale. (7-20-08)

"I am in your life now, resurrected as Sean. I have come into your life to teach you love, caring and gentleness. Do not concern yourself with how you appear to others. I asked to be borne of you and Kevin. I am teaching you continued merriment and laughter as I burst with joy! You have had a serious loss in your current lifetime, but I am here to help you overcome the heaviness, if you will let me. Relax, Sweet One, and know that we were together in Atlantis in another lifetime. You were not my mother, but a sibling. We worked hard and laughed often. I am in your current lifetime to bring you joy, laughter and unconditional love. Go forth and seize the day, as it is filled with all good things from Source."

As I mentioned earlier, I've got some proof that Sean was one of the lost children of Atlantis – and now it seems, through this writing with "Sean," that I too am one of these children! The knowledge we share in our subconscious minds may be part of the reason we have incarnated together in this lifetime. This awareness brings me to a loving place in time where I can acknowledge this fact and find solace.

It was many lifetimes ago that Atlantis was part of the Earth plane. It has been centuries since this continent was covered in water, holding its mysteries close to its energy. This energy has not revealed itself to the world yet, but this land mass is believed to be deep in the ocean. Sean and I have been together in many lifetimes, but since the existence of Atlantis was not believed during those time periods, we've never had the opportunity – until this lifetime – to share our stories.

I am seeking work and am asking the Universe about the latest job offer. (7-21-08)

"It is I, Amadeus, bringing love to you this day from the Universe. Your question seems to be about the job offer. Continue to delve into its potential. It seems like a possible fit. You can also continue to interview, as you left the door open.

"You alone will know if it is right. You alone know your abilities and your destiny. You are following a journey written many years ago, before you entered the Earth plane this time. I know you know that. You are a part of a bigger picture. You will be traveling safely by car or plane and will enjoy many books. Take note of suggestions and read those titles. Now, Sweet One, seize the day and put lazy energy at bay."

You see, I still have my own decisions to make. I've learned that I'm not able to get all the answers I want from others. It's up to me to continue to do the work to make my life what I want it to be. Each one of us has free will. If you get a reading from a psychic, know that it's based on the energy of the day, and you can change the outcome by changing the energy around anything that does not resonate positively with you. I am repeating this because it deserves attention, and so that you don't walk where you don't want to go. Change the energy and rearrange the direction of your life.

I didn't take any of the jobs offered to me that summer, but went into real estate with Kevin instead, and we have earned a nice living. I wasn't meant to get back into the horrible work conditions often found in the design industry, and many industries, for that matter. We now make our

Frances Pullin

own hours and take our breaks as needed. Currently, I spend three days a week volunteering for the School of Multidimensional Healing Arts and Sciences in Irvine, California. That gives me time in the morning for meditation, walks, breakfast, real estate, and being with Kevin.

Chapter Twenty Two

A Day in the Life of a Channel: Me

It is I, Amadeus, Sweet One. We on the Other Side are so pleased with your writing. You are allowing your audience into your life with this book, but are letting them know how such an ordinary day can become quite beautiful with a simple meditation and writing in your journal. You have shown them that it does not take superhuman powers to know your Guides and Others. How beautiful for those who are grieving to know that their loved ones are truly with them. You tell of writing with these loved ones and how they affect your life. Your generosity of sharing overwhelms us as we hear your take unfold through your own words.

Go in love, Amadeus.

A typical day finds me rising to greet the morning with a song in my heart. I thank the Universe for the beauty of all that I see! I head out and walk the hills in my neighborhood for twenty or thirty minutes and immerse myself in the sounds of the birds, the breeze, and the voices of my Guides. I return home for a quiet meditation and to do some writing in my journal. This is when I do my automatic writing with whomever wants to chat with me that day; it's how the teachings in this book were revealed to me.

There are days when I write for five minutes, and others when I write for half an hour or more. I like to write a question before I begin my meditation, and it is answered afterward by the appropriate entity. It's usually Amadeus, but it could be my son, my mother, or any of the Others who are with me and loving me. They are helping me on my journey. This is my time. It is part of the morning that I devote to loving me and nurturing my soul, as I have been taught to do by Them. Soon after, I blend up a nice green drink and curl up with a book to read while I nourish my body healthily.

On Tuesday and Thursday I work from 10-4 at the School of Multidimensional Healing Arts and Sciences. I stay at the school after 4:00 p.m. to meditate and grab a bite to eat with one of my fellow teachers before classes begin.

At 6:30 p.m., I begin to register the students arriving for evening classes; then I either join a class or teach one of my own. On the first and third Tuesday of each month, I lead a Spiritual Conversations forum. We discuss anything spiritual that the group wants to delve into – the nature of Spirit, energy healing, the radiation crisis at Fukushima, Japan, or any number of topics. There are some evenings when we view a movie on a spiritual subject. On the second and fourth Tuesday, I teach an Automatic Writing and Channeling class.

What fun I have teaching others and watching their first steps as they conquer meditation, channeling or automatic writing! There's a thrill inside me as I observe their growth on their spiritual path. On Thursday evenings, I rotate between "Mediumship Development," led by Debra, "Writing with Your Dream Muse," headed by Marjorie Miles, and "Seven Crystals for Seven Chakras," taught by Debi McKee. These are all seasoned, professional instructors who hold their classes in a love-and-laughter-filled atmosphere. I am proud to join their circle of proficiency!

On Saturday, I open the school for classes, teach mine, and if there's an interesting class later that day, I attend it. If not, I'm off to shop or play at whatever fuels my soul. That's my current schedule, which I expect will change as I grow spiritually and professionally, and I share it to show what a day in my life is like. Of course, I continue to study and hone my gifts, which have brought me to this point where I have become a teacher. This book is my gift to you.

As I write this chapter about a typical day, I have to include many hours that run late into the night. (My editor and I are both night owls and do our best work after 10:00 p.m.) When I'm not writing, teaching or channeling, I enjoy time with my family, just as I'm sure you do with yours. Birthdays, holidays, vacations, weddings and births are all a part of my life. And yes, death is also a part of our family time. We celebrate the lives of those who have gone before us as we grieve and heal together.

As you can see, I'm an ordinary woman living an extraordinary life and giving untold thanks to the Universe and its blessed contribution to my journey. Finding spirituality and making it a part of my life is one of the many gifts from the Universe. You too, dear reader, can create your own amazing journey just by putting one foot in front of the other on your personal path and practicing what I am teaching you.

Chapter Twenty Three

Truth in Truth

It is I, Amadeus. Truth is an ultimate place in trust. Truth is of utmost importance when dealing with anyone on the Earth plane. Once trust is broken by lack of truth, there is no turning back. Keep your Truth; it is your essence and your power.

Love, Amadeus.

What is the meaning of Truth as written above? (7-22-08)

"It is I, Amadeus. Truth is trust of God. God's pure light is the one and only Truth. When you meet with us, we share God's words with you and thus we are able to bring you truth from God's light, as we have been taught. Go forth and trust that which you speak to be of God's light: Truth as we teach it to you. To understand this, the following channeled definitions are important for you to know:

1. Perspective: self-assessment that lets you know where you stand in your spiritual development.
2. Ego: a heartfelt expression of who you are at any given moment.
3. Truth: an eternal concept that cannot be denied by man.
4. Spiritual Truth: the light that shines through your soul.

5. *Universal Truth: the deepest truth within you; comes only from "rebirthing," which means remembering what it was like before you incarnated in this lifetime.*
6. *Higher Self: the part of you that holds all knowledge of the Universe.*
7. *Integrity: a character trait that evolves from truth. "Walk the walk and talk the talk."*

This information came in this session from all Guides and Others who write with me. There was no more information that day, and no goodbye. Question this information. Turn it around in your mind, research it, and then reach out to me. As I have said before, I do want you to question the words written here – and everywhere.

What deeper level of trust are you ready for me to hear? (8-12-08)

"Your truth is from God only, my friend. You seek truth and wisdom far beyond your peers. It is not easy for you to feel you can share the truth of others. You walk ever afraid that you will not be able to read energy for them or channel for them. Truth comes from inside of you. Walk unafraid, as we are all here to love you and guide you as you go forward in truth and love of us and self. You must become truth and you will be unafraid. Share truth with others. Go with God's pure light and love. The trust will set you free. Love from all."

In early 2012, I became my truth. I was at lunch with people I didn't know, who, like me, were attending a conference in Los Angeles. After we'd ordered our meal and were chatting, I was asked what I did. It was a networking program, so the question did not surprise me. We were all interested in what the others did to make a living, and what had brought us together.

I freely stated that I was a channel. The information came boldly from my mouth, and it was too late to retrieve it! What had I just done? I had spoken my truth and now I bleakly awaited a reaction. The gentleman who asked the question continued by asking me what that meant exactly. He was curious, unafraid, and seemed to partially understand what I was telling him. He was looking for clarity for what he thought he knew about the subject. That was the first time I had ever stated my truth to a stranger. I was certainly excited to have it received without judgment.

After lunch, this man's wife came to chat with me. I told her that that was the first time I had stated in public that I was a channel, and I was excited to have it received without judgment. During the afternoon break, I was again approached by the wife. She was beaming with delight after sharing my news with her husband. He said he was proud to know me. We shed a tear, hugged and finished our program. I had touched someone with my honesty.

Do you see why there has been so much writing about "truth" in my journals? My Guides and I knew I was still in hiding, but since that life-changing lunch break, I tell whoever asks about what I do and who I am, the truth. And I even tell some who *don't* ask! I'm not looking for a reaction; it's because I'm no longer afraid and am honored to be me.

You may question the account above regarding tears during the afternoon break, but let me explain: I am an Empath. There are many of us who are empathetic walking the Earth plane. We have psychic abilities, and we soak up psychic information – the energy and emotions of others. We have a deep understanding of other people's energy, and are patient, asking many questions. We tend to be sensitive to animals and negative newscasts; in fact, we prefer not to watch TV news or read a newspaper. If we do glance at a paper, we skim it for positive stories, savoring these delightful pieces of information, as they give us pleasure and joyous tears.

I didn't always know this about myself and thus spent much time immersed in other people's negative energy. As hard as I worked on staying in positive energy, it was being taken from me by myself and my inability to move out of adverse power. But once I learned to recognize that I was an Empath, a few years ago, I was able to protect myself from the absorption of negativity by surrounding myself with white light from Source. Sometimes I'm still unaware of the energy of those souls around me, but am growing more conscious of it all the time. Everything I am learning takes discipline, attention and practice.

In my dream, I was dancing with Amadeus through the grass on the knoll. Joy and happiness were what I was feeling, but why was I crying? I had no idea why there were tears when I was feeling such joy. (8-20-08)

"It is I, Amadeus.

"The tears were of your happiness. Love, love, love. You are no longer sad, but always joyful in the world. You are causing others to feel the laughter and mirth, chasing away all sadness. Joy in the world! May peace follow you all of your days on the Earth plane."

Amadeus, what are these gifts I have put into my heart from past lifetimes? (8-30-08)

"It is I, Amadeus, Sweet One. This has been very powerful for you. You have chosen seeds from past lives that will manifest in joy in your life. You have chosen psychic ability to arise at much higher levels. You have no fear of this work you are doing. It will become greater with each day. Do not take this lightly. You will continue to heal others. You have brought joy, which will bring you the riches you are seeking. Go forth in love and light. Rid yourself of this current job offer and use this new energy to manifest that which we are bringing to you. We have been leading you to this day, Sweet One. Go in peace. Go in inner peace. Love, light and laughter, Amadeus."

The riches I am seeking are found deep in my soul. I am seeking to bring others the knowledge of the Light of Source and self-love. I want all who wish to partake to grab a piece of my knowledge, question it, find it to be authentic, and then follow it.

I have been shown that my work is in this psychic community, not in a job which would please others around me. Those around me include my friends, family, and even my husband. They don't understand that

I am different than they are. They hear me and honor me, but do not begin to feel the depth of my longing to continue my work in the spiritual community. They think that riches only come in the form of money and nice things. Don't get me wrong. We all need money to survive, and I am surrounded by fine things. But now it is time to rise with the riches which are found in my soul and in my heart.

What is the true meaning of grief and what does it teach us? (9-10-08)

"Yes, it is I, Amadeus. You have had your share of grief, Sweet One. Friends, parents, and ultimately your son have brought you to a space in life where you chose this spiritual world. You have felt that grief is a selfish emotion, and that it is. Grief is not selfish in a negative way, but in love that is being expressed. It teaches us that our time on the Earthly plane should be spent wisely, lovingly, and spiritually. If you lift the veil of grief, you will learn of the wondrous joy of the Universe. Those who have transitioned during your current incarnation are joyously celebrating the day when you will join them. Do not inflict pain on others. Love with light and purity, Sweet One. The tears are an earthly creation, and you will find they lessen as you grow in spirit. Go then, and be at peace, knowing one day your work here will be done, and you will dwell with those you grieve for. Know too, Sweet One, you may grieve the child in you who had lessons to learn. Know that you are still learning and will continue until the death of your current incarnate. Love from all, Amadeus."

After this writing with Amadeus, I continued to write. The information came from the "Others," but in the end I arrived at a simple conclusion as to what I was being taught during this writing. That conclusion is as follows: *You are healed in layers. You agreed to be a part of this. You are a complex entity. Serial killers do not grieve.*

Then I continued to write what I had been taught about grief:

1. Grief is created out of death or loss of some kind. It could be the loss of a home to fire or burglary, or any personal violation.

2. Grief is filled with pain, sadness and confusion, but it is not of pain alone.
3. Grief's function is to help us reach deep levels of emotional truth; it guides us to take personal responsibility for our physical being with love and spiritual direction.
4. Grief teaches us about love by showing us how deeply we cared for the person who left us.
5. Grief brings about a time to write and acts as a portal that's essential to our spiritual process.

Your Higher Angelic Self's DNA can be activated when it's triggered by your expression of grief through tears or just sadness. By "Angelic Self," I mean your Higher Self – these words can be used interchangeably. Your Angelic or Higher Self is that part of you that has been with your soul through many incarnations. Some of your Guides and Angels may come and go, but your Higher Angelic Self always remains with the soul that is you.

Travel to the moment in time when grief caused your DNA's Angelic Self to be activated. To heal this, I suggest having a past life regression session with a licensed hypnotherapist or someone who has been trained in this skill. You may learn some surprising things.

The tragic loss of my son and others dear to me has brought with it momentous growth in both my love for others and my spirituality. And it's caused me to be filled with the truth of who I am. This spiritual growth has brought forth a greater understanding of mankind. I'm able to witness the kindness of a stranger and know that they're meant to be on my path that day to teach me the beauty in all that Source has created. I also have a greater understanding of why I shouldn't judge others. If I haven't spoken to them and heard their story, then who am I to judge? And if I *have* heard their story, then why would I feel entitled to criticize them? I'm constantly asking, "How do I want to be perceived in this lifetime?" I wouldn't want my actions judged by anyone, but particularly by someone who does not know my story. I want to be remembered for a quick smile and a listening ear. I don't want to be thought of as that critic who acted negatively in the presence of others.

I've walked a long path, and the journey has not been without trials and tribulations. I've risen to the top of my game, so to speak, and I'm a more fully-developed soul for having taken this trek. And while I know that there's much more to learn and a long way to travel, I move forward in life now knowing I am surrounded by truth, beauty and the love of others in my energy field and beyond.

Do not, by any means, believe that I know all and have become a perfect specimen. No way! I have, however, gained much more clarity as to how Source sees perfection, and that gives me much more to strive toward. I can see some of the love that I've been asked to bring to the table of my family and friends, and how I've been asked to teach and share with others.

On a walking meditation, I met Isaiah for the first time. Isaiah appears to me as a Guide. On this day I asked who was with me and for what reasons. (9-18-08)

"I am Isaiah. You are correct, Little One. Your grief that sent you so boldly to us was the death of your son. You, Wee One, have been searching for us for many years. You were in your twenties when you first began to dabble in the unknown. It was the death of your family as you knew it that first brought you sniffing. Your initial family home was not a loving one always, but you held onto it. (This takes us all the way back to my childhood and first marriage, when I had moved from my family's home in Tucson to Yuma, Arizona. My darling daughter was born there, but we left when she was three weeks old, as my then-husband, Steve, had been discharged from the Marine Corps.) *When you returned home from Yuma, your childhood home was up for sale and the birth family was split into different locations. Sisters Marilyn and Pat had already moved to California years earlier. The remainder of your birth family was moving to Sacramento, as your father was promoted and orchestrated the move. You were left alone in Tucson with your husband and*

new baby, Michelle. You did not even realize the depth of your grief over your initial family's seeming desertion. Thus, you were left to grow as a child with a child. It was then that your distrust of men came into being. They could shake the very foundation of the family. And they did!

"Steve, your husband at the time, took on long hours working for a burglar alarm company. Damon was conceived, but was not entirely a blessing at the time. There you were with a full time job and two children. You quit your job and tried to manage the household by bringing in other people's children to love and support and to bring money to the family unit. It was a stressful time with bill collectors calling and a husband absent most of the time. It was then you knew that with inner strength you could end this marriage and care for your children with the love only you seemed to have for them. Life in that family unit had also closed its door due to a man's aloofness. Your parents had returned to Tucson, but did not support a divorce in the family.

"This was extremely difficult for you, as you had promised as a young girl to only lie with one man. You had promised God and had disappointed God deeply. You did not understand that you were learning a lesson that you and Steve and the children had agreed to long before their conception. They chose the two of you to learn the lesson of love having no bounds. They lost him, but they retained you, and you were their life source.

"After a dating relationship failed, we brought Kevin to you. He is perfect for you, and you for him. He loved Damon and Michelle as his own and one day adopted them, as he had stood in for many days, weeks, months and years as their father. Steve had remarried soon after the divorce and had moved on with his new family and child. So it is that we advise you to love Kevin, laugh with him, and keep him until death do you part. You opened a new chapter together. You conceived Kevin II and Sean and raised them alongside of Michelle and Damon with love and abandonment.

"Now, for the first time, just the two of you live in your home. Enjoy it! Revel in it! Love deeply and enjoy the day! With love from all of us, Isaiah."

It was quite shocking to read about the sadness I felt when my parents moved the family home to Sacramento. I had never faced that situation with anything but a knowledge that life was moving forward, and yet that incident set the tone for my feelings of loneliness, which continue, at times, to this day. I thank my Guides for digging deep and bringing meaning to this and many situations I have never understood before.

I have always thanked my children for choosing me to be their parent. All through life, I've had a strong feeling that it was their choice to have me as their mother, and through my spiritual studies and the classes I've taken, I've found this to be pleasantly true. Isaiah does not visit often, yet his job was clearly handled with that lengthy writing.

What news do you have for me today? (9-21-08)

"It is I, Amadeus, Sweet One. You are moving in the right direction, although any direction is better than none. I like the peacefulness that seems to be setting in. Getting the house in order and repairing things that have weighed you down for many years is very important. You are feeling free of "mother's burdens" with the children grown and out of the house and are able to take care of fixing all. This in turn makes you feel less burdened. The closet is almost cleaned and we brought it up many months ago as a symbol of being ready without burden to move into a new home when it shows up for you. To go off each day into the work realm knowing the job at home is done. You now face an empty nest knowing that there are children who love you and whom you love. Also, you have a husband with whom you are laughing. You are ready, Sweet One. Go forth in love, Amadeus."

And then, more came from Isaiah during the same writing:

"Yes, I, Isaiah will be with you for now. When you were quite small, you were abused. Physically and mentally. This has been mentioned to you before, even as your memory does not bring it forth. You do not have to relive the details; just know it was. This is another piece of the puzzle as to the "control by men" issues. It is a part of your DNA now, and you are here on this plane in this lifetime to rid yourself of the desire to control. When you lose control, you check out. Stay with us, dear child, and don't check out. It is time for continued personal growth, and you are at a pinnacle to grow in leaps and bounds. Go now, grow now under our wings of love, Isaiah."

So, as you can see, once again I am being disciplined somewhat for not moving forward, and then applauded when I do. I like this positive experience. You will also see that my control issues have surfaced again, and I appear not to remember all of the abuse that I went through. I know my parents' move to Tucson when I was quite young helped to save me from a young man who visited my family's home often during the sixth year of my life, when the family was living in Alaska. I did have a sweet little girl crush on him and imagine, but do not know for sure, that he is a part of this. We supposedly ask for these things to happen for a reason, and I have learned that it has made me a very strong woman who does not want to be controlled by anyone or anything.

Tell me about something I don't remember, but know it affects me to this day, as I try to always be behind the wheel of the car wherever I am going. (9-28-08)

"Yes, Wee One. It is again Isaiah who will help you here. You were very small when this began. You are one of many children to be brought forth by your mother who loves you, Esther. Your father was away at school to become an air traffic controller and she, without a license, was driving you and your three sisters to the store. (This was in Los Alamos, New Mexico, where I was born and where we lived for just a few years.) *Your mother's car accident could have ended all of your lives, but it did not happen. You stopped the car with your Angelic Being. You and your sisters were saved by blending together with your mother in an instant. You did not go off the road, as you had made the decision that there was to be much more of life. Yes, that is why you and your sisters don't make good passengers. It seems to me you are healing, as Jarod has explained to me that you are not to fear again.* (Remember, I call Jarod, who appeared to me as a policeman, my "Guardian Angel of Car Accidents.") *He is taking care of your soul during all of your new incarnates. So, Wee One, you are now aware of when your Angelic Self emerged and you became you. Loving, caring, and selfless. Go forth with love in your heart and love all that life here on this Earth plane has to offer. Lovingly loving you, Isaiah*

It is I, Amadeus

I must say now that I didn't remember many of these writings until I began to transcribe them to share with you. This is one of those scripts. I have faith in it, since it's true that the four of us girls (under the age of eight) were in that car, and it was given to me by Isaiah from the Other Side. Some of the things that I've learned along this path have been questioned and rationalized, but this passage and any others from my Guides or Angels come without question. Who am I to question Source or its blessings in the form of my teachers on the Other Side? I question man, not Source.

We are back together this morning, and I am wondering how long you have been with me. (10-22-08)

"It is I, Amadeus. For centuries we have worked with you to bring you to this place in time when you would know us and accept us and bring us forward in your life. We are all here to help you spread Source's light and love to all who know you so that they too can understand the message that we bring to the Earth plane. Do not be frightened of your gift. It is God-given. Your gifts are of love, joy, laughter, and abundance. Your words will affect the Earth plane and its inhabitants for centuries to come. We protected you in this lifetime so that you could mature, nurture, and gain the trust of those whom you will teach. Go forward and do God's will. Love from all of us."

Notice please, that I have been asked by my Guides and Angels not to be frightened of my gift. Here you must know that I have completed many past life regressions where I go into trance with a healer or hypnotherapist and visit a past lifetime. It hasn't been pretty going back to the days of castles and beyond. I have seen many things that were done to me because of this gift that I have always been proud to use. It's been my downfall until this incarnation, but now it appears that this book and you, the reader, will help make it an offering that affects the lives of many in the coming centuries. Remember, it came from Source, so I trust it.

Frances Pullin

Who is with me today and what do you have to tell? (10-29-08)

"Good morning! It is Justine. You are going in so many directions: channeling, Theta Healing, Reiki, and more. We find it wonderful. There is no time like the present. Remember, you are in your current digs to work with Frances keeping the outside out for now. Your friend Laura has many things to say and tell you. Keep focused on the positive. You are to teach of God's love in word and in action. Nurture Frances so she can nurture others. You are coming to a pinnacle in your life. Write down your business guidelines so you have an organized picture for others to assist you. You are moving forward in joy, self-confidence and abundance.

"Kevin is getting started, and he will go far. You will stand beside him when the loss of his mother weighs him down. He has done everything a son can do to reassure her of his love. Go forth with him in love and light. Take no ill will. She has loved you as a daughter for many years now. She made it to the celebrations and now is tired and ready to be with the Source. In love and light, Justine."

Only four months earlier, in June, Kevin's mother, Eleanor, had joined us for Kevin II and Amy's wedding. Five of her six children were present with their spouses, and she told me how proud she was of the way her children had grown up. They looked so handsome, and she was noticing their good manners. She so appreciated what they had become, to themselves and to each other.

That Sunday, after the wedding, we had a birthday party for her. At the age of 90, we celebrated her life and her accomplishments. We had a delicious dinner in our backyard, with my sisters-in-law trying to do all of the cooking so I could enjoy the party. I so relish being part of this loving family! It was that year, at Thanksgiving time, that Eleanor Johnson Pullin left to join her husband in the presence of Source. Kevin's mother is remembered with love and a deep sense of caring, as family always came first to her then, as I'm sure it does now.

I am feeling stuck and would like some help to move forward.

(11-9-08)

"It is Justine, and I am here to tell you to move forward. I know you will, as this is time for movement for you. You will continue to explore side ventures, albeit ever so slowly. Your real estate will become a reality. You will become the star that you are. Kevin, too, will do well. Most importantly, during this time, his toy cars must sell, as they are no longer needed. Do this and you will prosper. Go in peace, Sweet Angel. Justine."

Kevin and I have done well in real estate, and we will continue. It is a tough time to be starting out, as it is a down market and there is very little inventory, but it's also a good time to be starting out because there's so much to learn. We're also discovering that not everyone has the same sense of right and wrong as we do, so it can be difficult when we have to deal with those who don't believe in truth and honesty.

As much as Kevin does not agree with everything I do and say in regard to spiritualism, he is the most trustworthy and honest man I have ever known. Yes, there are times when I say to him, "Don't tell me what to do!" but that's usually in response to petty remarks about when to make a turn when driving and other such nonsense. My Guides and Spirits put him in my life for a reason – so I can learn to trust men. I trust him with all that I have in my heart, and all that I am. Plus, I am to learn patience from this kind man.

I am saddened at the loss of Kevin's mother. I am alone today in my grief, without my husband beside me or me with him. He is in Florida, and I will not be making the trip. Can you send me some comfort? (11-25-08)

"It is I, Amadeus. You are grieving and rightly so. The woman you grew to love has left you. You will not meet again on the Earth plane. This is the will of God. You will be tender with her son. This is a sad time in his life. Kevin chooses you, as you are like her but not like her. You will make your long drive to Tucson alone and reflect on your lifetime with her. We will, of course, join you on your journey."

Justine took her turn with this sadness:

"Your son was with you last night to bring comfort at this troubling time. He will always hover nearby and sometimes will let you know. Be happy with her transition to the Other Side. Go in peace and love this day that Source has bestowed upon you. Love, Justine."

Again, Amadeus:

"It is I, Amadeus. I wish to speak again, There is grief and mourning. The mother of Kevin is of God and her soul has turned back to the Light. I wish to say I love you. Goodbye for now."

Justine had stepped out of the way for Amadeus to send his love. Then she was back.

"It is again Justine. We all wish for you to work hard. Ready yourself for the next step of your journey. No, do not forget your dream of yesterday, but put it in place. You will need contacts for your business. Both businesses, but one client will come and feed the second business. You are blessed, Sweet One, and you will prosper in the coming year and lifetime. Lovingly, Justine."

Here, Justine is referring to my real estate success and that I might find clients in my pursuit of spirituality. This has happened, and I am blessed with clients. I wasn't with Kevin in Florida, but in Arizona, where we had planned to have Thanksgiving. I was to fly to Florida for a visit with his mother after Kevin had had a few days with her; then we would travel back to Arizona to have Thanksgiving with my sister and her family. But that wasn't to be, as she had chosen her time to leave. Kevin arrived after midnight in Florida and was to visit his mother the next day, but in the early hours of the morning, the call came from the hospital that she had passed just two hours earlier. We all have the choice of when we go, and Kevin was not to speak with her. He did go to the hospital with his brother that morning to kiss her cheek one last time.

Death is a beautiful thing to the soul who is moving on, but can bring about such sadness to those of us left behind. Many months later, his mother came through in a reading to tell me of her love for me and how she wished she had been more vocal about it during her lifetime. Of course, she has nothing to apologize for, as I felt the love and knew I was taking great care of her first-born son.

Chapter Twenty Four

A New Year, 2009

It is I, Amadeus. There will always be another year in front of you, so long as you exist on the Earth plane. Each year will bring new trials, tribulations and joys! You will face all of these emotions with strength and courage. We will be with you and support you at all times.

Love, Amadeus.

There is a new year in front of me.
What do you know about this new year? (1-4-09)

"It is I, Amadeus. Welcome to a wonderful new year where you will run with your business in real estate and in your channeling classes. You have been thinking of a number to charge for your sessions. Let us work together. If you give away your gift without an exchange, it has no value to you or to those who seek assistance from you. It will be valueless for those who come. You are ready and need to believe in yourself. What you request for your services as far as compensation must be adequate to the soul seeking information for them to trust your worthiness."

"Many things were revealed to you this week. Eleanor, your husband's mother, knew of your spirituality in the end of her lifetime. I believe she, as well as Damon, will assist you on this journey. Listen for them and for us. There are many to make this successful for you and those you will

love. You begin to bring light back into the lives of those who seek your guidance. Go, Sweet One, and begin the next part of your journey. Love, Amadeus."

So it is that my Guides and Angels know when I am not asking for adequate compensation in return for the blessings that many souls will receive. There are those who cannot pay, and I will weigh that; but more often I have found that people do not want a gift, as they want to respect the information received. In order to gain this respect, they are willing to give fair compensation.

What direction should I be taking at this time? (2-16-09)

"It is I, Amadeus. You know what to work on. Give up your fear of failure – or is it your fear of success? Go forth in your business endeavors. You are the leader here. Let no one else bend you. You have the gifts, knowledge and strength. Go forward with them. In love and light we love you, Amadeus."

This was a very brief writing. At times, my Guides are very direct and to the point. I have often struggled with the fear of success. Even as I began to develop this book, I was suffering from trepidation. Finally, with much meditation and soul searching, I determined that it was the anxiety of becoming successful that was holding me back from getting this book into print.

This publication may take me places where I am uncomfortable and feel unsure of myself. For example, I will need to promote it, and that is territory I have never investigated. Also, you will either enjoy or condemn this book. That, too, I must be ready to endure, though I truly believe, in the deepest recesses of my heart, that there will be little condemnation. If you were drawn to read this material, then you are open to receiving, questioning and researching it. I honor that you will continue to read more and voraciously devour many other books on the subjects that are touched on here.

A few weeks ago, I channeled for a small audience during the Holistic Faire and Marketplace at SMHAS. To my amazement, as I finished, I was applauded! I believe this is part of my apprehension. Simply stated: stage fright. I know that the audiences will grow, and that I must remain humble and dedicated. I must continue to honor my gift as I move through this upcoming transition in my life.

I have had readings from many psychics and intuitive people. Their chatter about the success of this book and its gift to you has made me uneasy. Even my family in Spirit are sending messages letting me know it's time to dream bigger than I ever have – and thus, stage fright looms. And yet I'm learning, even as I write this, that my Guides and Angels are here to take care of me through the applause from those who enjoy my ideas and want to embrace them, and the disdain from those who fear my teaching due to their limited belief system. I am to stand on my own two feet, hold my Guides and Angels close, and move rapidly forward.

I am aware, too, that I need to keep Ego in check. I won't know the result of my accomplishment until the book is in your hands, you are reading my words, and ever so gently turning its pages. Perhaps you will view it onscreen via the latest gadget from the electronic media. However this information reaches you, I am proud that I am being allowed to share all that I've learned. I wish to be your teacher and have you as my students.

What is my secret message of the day? (3-4-09)

"Yes, it's Mathilda with an 'h'! You are rediscovering your spiritual path, and it will be fun! You will continue on this path for a lifetime. Skip through the forest, run on the beach, swim the seven oceans, if only in your mind. Keep your glass half full, as always, and go in peace and love."

Next, Amadeus brought in his views:

"It is I, Amadeus. Do as Mathilda suggests. You are so loved and special in the eyes of all of your newfound friends and family. There are no jealousies, and when negative energy comes your way you will send it packing. You are loved for you and appreciated for what you bring to the table. Want not and go in peace."

After a brief pause, the message continued...

"It is yet again Amadeus. You and I are back in mid-century England again. You recognize the people from your healing in this past life where you hugged the abused stable boy. You did not see this boy during this current past life regression session, as he was healed with that hug you gave to him. You are to go forward and heal as you have done before. Love, Light, and Blessings, Amadeus."

During a past life regression session in early 2009, I found myself in mid-century England. I was employed by the King and one day wandered outside the castle. There, I came upon a stable boy, crying and shivering in the cold of winter. I reached out and gave him the jacket I was wearing. As I wrapped it about his shoulders, I gave him a loving, warm embrace. He was quite astounded, and his tears dried on his beautiful face. In his acceptance of my gift, his life was changed forever and he found the courage to move forward out of his position in life and into a new experience.

While reliving that life in England, I found that the streets were crowded with people and animals, but the smell of the animals and their waste in the cobblestone streets was not offensive to me. I'm amazed that I felt that way back then, because in this current lifetime, never having lived near farm animals, I gag with distaste at those smells.

As I looked around me, I saw children wildly running through the streets, as there were many orphans due to their parents' deaths or abandonment, and no one could care for these children. These orphans grew up without regard for others, as they had not been parented. I watched a small boy steal an apple from a vendor's cart; he was yelled at, and yet the vendor knew that because of the theft, the boy would have something to eat that day so he let him go on his way. Wow! That was powerful! These scenes seemed to light up and were vivid in my mind. Letting your imagination take in all that you see and feel during a past life regression brings you to the actual physical and mental experience of these lifetimes.

Past life regression is often practiced in the spiritual community, because often you can heal things making you uncomfortable in this lifetime by revisiting past lives. For example, if you are afraid of dogs, as I am, you might find out why and learn to control the fear through love of self and forgiveness of the situation that arose back then. In my case, I found that I've practiced spirituality in past lives in many societies that called it "witchcraft." Due to a lack of understanding by the people of that time and to church dogma, these teachings were labeled "black magic." (To my utter dismay, real witchcraft is still alive in some churches today.)

In another visit to a past life, I was chased out of the walled city I was living in by dogs and men on horseback in full armor. I ran through a meadow, but just at the edge of the forest I was caught by the throat by the dogs. I can relate this experience because a shaman put me in a hypnotic state and I relived it. It was painful, and I remember it vividly, but I am now able to walk up to dogs and pet them – though not without trepidation. I approach little dogs with friendliness and big dogs with these words in my mind: "I am safe." I can even pet the large dogs, though with some reservation, and I can understand how they are so completely loved by their owners. But before my session with this shaman, I would freeze in my tracks when a dog approached and pray for its owner to quickly appear.

I had originally booked this session with the shaman to try and determine why my hearing seems to be getting worse with time. I can say that it's just my family DNA, but I do not truly believe that theory and was choosing instead to learn of its origin for me, so that I can begin healing it. I am a channel, so feel that my hearing should be profound as I listen to questions from my audience.

When I relived this traumatic incident with the dogs tearing at my throat, I realized that this event in Europe centuries ago has followed me for lifetimes. And since our sinuses, ears, and throat are connected, I felt that the damage to my throat long ago might be interfering with my hearing during this lifetime. Now I am choosing to work on this issue and have my hearing reinstated without help from the medical community, if at all possible. Do not misunderstand me in regard to the medical community. I believe that there is purpose in what doctors and nurses do, and I respect them. I do not, however, believe that all that ails you can *only* be cured with a prescription for the latest drug on the market. And so, in meditation, I picture myself in settings where there is ambient noise, yet I hear conversations with my friends quite clearly. This is what the shaman told me to practice, and I do it as often as I can

At this time, I'd like to explain what I know about Shamanism. A shaman is a conduit between the spirit world and the Earth plane, and there are many types: healers, medicine men and women, and messengers. Shamans get information when they travel in the three worlds: upper, middle and lower. The word "shamanism" is originally from Siberia, where shamans are also known as healers. Shamans are found all over the world and have practiced energy medicine for over 35,000 years. In the Western world, many of them are influenced by Peruvian, Native American and Hawaiian traditions. They journey in other dimensions and call out to the spirit world, using rattles, drums, bells and chants to assist them. I love their passion for what they do and their love of nature and all things of the earth.

According to my shaman friend, Cheryl Gall, a shaman reaches an altered state of mind through sacramental procedures and/or rituals which enable him or her to connect with Spirit. They practice various types of ceremonies that may involve past life and present-day soul retrieval, releasing old stories, healings, and entity extractions. Shamans are known as cleaners, as they remove psychic debris released from the energetic body. (Psychic debris is energy that may be picked up from doing a healing on a person or doing a reading.) They can also pick up debris from clearing a space or from clearing a blockage that has manifested in the physical body. Many people report that after working with a shaman, their injury, sickness or disease has been removed, and that there's a feeling of lightness. This in turn helps the healed soul receive clarity on its path in life.

Past life regressions can be done by many practitioners, but I prefer a shaman or hypnotherapist. There's lots of material on shamanism that you can explore, if you're interested. If you are afraid of dogs, as I was, you might find out why from a past life and learn to control the fear through love of self and letting go of traumatic events in that lifetime.

You can also revisit the past in your current life experience. I have done this and recommend it highly, as we can often heal the present by visiting the past – whether in this lifetime or a previous one. Please enjoy a book on this subject: *Healing the Present from the Past: The Personal Journey of a Past Life Researcher*, written by my colleague and valued friend, Dr. Heather S. Friedman Rivera.

What work do I have ahead of me now? (3-10-09)

"It is Justine. Your work has begun. Your Angel will be yours, and you will begin to heal others. We will be with you. We will enable you to go forward, as you have done before and are capable of doing. You have many fires, and you will become prosperous once more. Go, follow your heart. Grow and learn and return here for more meditation and much-needed love. Justine."

It was on this day that the name of my new business endeavor was revealed to me. It's called Angels Healing Hearts. When I was ready to set up a website, I found that name had been taken, but Angels-Healing-Hearts.com was available, so I purchased it instead.

I sat peacefully in meditation, and when it was ended, I wrote the following: (3-18-09)

"It is I, Amadeus. You are powerful and possess many gifts. People are gravitating to you because you stand in the Light, Sweet One. Stand tall and strong and lead them. Know you can do this. Know you are also a people-keeper. It is recognized by the genuine love, joy and peace in your face. Go forth, Sweet One, and teach of God's love." (I had once coined the phrase "people-keeper" for myself and a dear friend, because we both hold on to people and relationships as long as we are able. Amadeus, who has been with me always, was aware of this.)

Next, Jarod spoke:

"It is Jarod, your Guardian Angel. You are correct and need to see your doctor. Something is not right. Follow your instincts. Make tomorrow a day for you. Go in health this day."

Frances Pullin

At this point in time, I don't remember the malady that caused me to visit my doctor, but it is beautiful that when Spirit feels the need for medical assistance, my Friends do not hesitate to suggest it. I ignore what the doctor has to say if I feel it does not serve me, but in this case I'm sure I listened, as I was directed by my Angel to "go forth in health."

Chapter Twenty Five

Ancestors Revealed

It is I, Amadeus. Greetings to you, Sweet One. Today we will talk with you about your ancestry. Your DNA is filled with many souls who have been with you throughout your entire journey. They leave and then return. They come at times as mother, father, sister, brother, aunt, uncle or friend. Know that they are key in your development as you move through each phase of each journey. Revel in their energy.

Love, Amadeus.

What part do our ancestors play in our spiritual evolution, and why do they matter in our current human experience? What can you tell me about the plane that they are on, and what deems them "ancestors" versus "deceased loved ones"? (3-30-09)

"Your ancestors are the fringe of your being, so to speak, to assist in bringing your past together. They have been watching from the sidelines, readying to join you in thoughts or dreams to assist you on this journey. As you love a recently deceased soul, so too have you known and have loved an ancestor on a different plane.

"The plane that the ancestors reside on is inside the Earth and centered by energy. The energy can be recreated as a human entity, but not necessarily to you in this lifetime. You may carry the features of ancestors,

but that is but a grounding tool for the soul energy. It may not have anything to do with the lessons your soul is learning in this lifetime. Dear One, you are soul energy unto yourself, and if you accept this truth here on this Earth plane, you will realize it is something you have been chosen to repair and heal while you are here. While you can consciously make a decision to heal, do so. Go forth and be you, and heal the you in you. Amadeus."

How powerful is that? I can't believe the information that's being gifted to me through those I cannot see! To reiterate: When information comes through my writings after meditation, I don't question the content or the messenger. How in the world could I be making this up? I can't for an instant believe that these words are not from my beloved Guides and Angels. Question if you will, as I have invited you to do, but know that I never question now.

Here is more information that flowed in that morning...

"I am Carl Sonnenberg. I am here to teach you many things. We will begin with your belief system. You have disregarded formal religions, yet you walk a spiritual path. Go forward on this path with love and light from us beyond any place you thought you might learn from. Go with knowing your ancestral DNA is actually filled with love of self – the lesson you have been guided to know. With that we shall speak again in truth."

I feel a familiar energy. Who is it that has come to connect with me today? (4-1-09)

"It is Carl Sonnenberg of your DNA and past lineage. You entered into this family of DNA many centuries ago. You have lived many lifetimes on the Earth plane, and we are thrilled with the new path you are on. It has been a part of you always. You did wonder in younger years how you knew of things you had not learned in books. You learned these things at the knee of great masters. Your lineage belongs to one of extreme intelligence, and you have chosen this path once again in this lifetime. You are reapplying tools of many yesteryears. You are working on, and continue to work on, love of self and self-worth. We have had a tremendous amount of injustice in our

DNA, and we are finding your self-worth to be gainly rewarding. Have you not been told you act superior to others? That is because your make-up has shown it to be true. Not in a coveting way, but in a loving and gifting way.

"*You have returned to be a teacher of love and life, self-respect and forgiveness of sins, past and present. I am here, as I have known you in your past incarnates. No matter where you have been, you do not draw a line with color. You are respecting those around you who need strength and teaching. You are here to turn our DNA to love. Go, Young One, and follow Source's light and mission for you. Love of family, Carl.*"

As Carl spoke, I realized I've been given a daunting task. I've been asked by Spirit to assist in healing atrocities perpetrated against particular branches of my family DNA. Through eons of time, we have been persecuted and ultimately killed just for being us. World War II found us being rounded up and disrespectfully piled in infernos, just because of our lineage.

In this lifetime I am more than a spiritual being, I'm a healer. At first, I felt I was meant to heal others in need of my services, but now it appears that I'm also to heal portions of family and ancestral DNA that goes back centuries in time and remove the pain from persecution by other races and religions. I will not take this task as oppressive. I *will* take it on with love and the conviction that I can make a difference in this world and in past lifetimes. I am proud to be part of my entire lineage, as it is filled with many cultures and beliefs.

I'd like you to know that I'm in possession of many family documents. Days after writing the above information, I went through them – and indeed, Carl Sonnenberg's name and photo was among the writings! Back in the early 1900s, he was part of a branch of our family.

I love what I'm being asked to do with regard to healing my family's DNA and I'll do it with every intention of love for all in my ancestry, from long ago to present day. I will be the catalyst to bring healing and love to generations past and to those yet to be born. I will find the right person to assist me in this endeavor of healing ancestral DNA through past-life regressions by interviewing hypnotherapists in my community. They will know exactly how to do this healing work.

Chapter Twenty Six

Moving Further Through Grief

It is I, Amadeus, Sweet One! You move so slowly and passionately through your grief. You are so connected to your son that it has been difficult for you to move forward. Know you are loved by us, and we will work with him to ease your sadness. We congratulate you on your progress thus far.

Love, Amadeus.

It is a grand and glorious day! Who will be chatting with me this day? (4-03-09)

"It is Mathilda with an 'h'! You are so peaceful. No worries. No fears. No, no, no, no, no, no. You are at peace, and you will be open to us this day. Move slowly as you cook a meal and savor with gratitude what you will learn. Damon did indeed want this experience for you. He is looking for more commitment. You will visit the bookstore again soon and will find me there and bring me home to swell with your other Angels and Fairies. It is I, Mathilda, in love and light."

A few hours after this message came through; I went to the local metaphysical bookstore and chose a fairy statue representing Mathilda from the shelf. The need to enter that bookstore has ended for now, but its doors will swing open again one day to welcome me inside. I brought the fairy home and gave it a prominent place in my living space.

I continue to pursue my spiritual journey, as Damon has requested. He chats with me and is always in the kitchen when I cook. We both love the creations I make. (He was famous in his circle of family and friends for his sweets: crème brûlée, chocolate mousse, and chocolate truffles.)

That afternoon, Sara popped into my writing with a loving message:

"We have all been concerned about you lately. Staying in, not enjoying walks. You have not loved your home or yourself for a while the way we wish for you. This is Sara, and I am wishing for this day to be cleansing and all about you. You have learned much this spring. Keep it up and let love and light be your guide throughout the day. Go in love and light and become busy with the work ahead of you. Lovingly from all, Sara."

This was the second message that day. Oh, they know me so well! They had watched and had felt my sadness. I know I must not let myself dwell on negativity, so it was perfect for these messages to take care of me. I don't remember what I did after my writing session, but I'm going to guess that I went into the kitchen and created a masterful dinner for my husband and I. Damon's passion for cooking was learned at my knee, and we both know that what makes us feel at peace is bringing bountiful meals to others.

These messages filled with love always bring joy to my heart, and later that day, dear Amadeus came back to be with me...

"It is I, Amadeus. Damon is always near. You will know it without knowing it. You will feel his vibration more often than ever. He knows his dad misses him each day and each time you gather without him. Look to this day! Amadeus."

What can I say? I do feel Damon's energy, and will look forward to hearing from him more often. It was closing in on the day of his birth in the month of April, and Amadeus knew just what I needed to make my heart sing. I thank these beautiful beings, as they love me with such abandonment.

This would have been Damon's 39th birthday. What heaviness I feel. How will I get through this day? How will I know my boy is safe?

(4-11-09)

"Hey, Ma! Yes, I am fine. I am happy. I love what you are learning. You will be so far advanced when you join me. I have the key to bring you here, but many moons will come and go and many suns will rise before that day. Tell everyone I love them and I know they miss me, but I am with them all. Have them choose a sign and look for it. It will be there. Your growth pleases all of us. Don't worry about the other children. They are on their own path. Take care of you. With everlasting love, Damon, as you know me."

Damon, the Spirit born to me and named by me. This was the first time he wrote with me. Reread his words – the love of a son to his mother, and yet, he finishes with "Damon, as you know me." He is reminding me that during our relationship in this lifetime, I knew him as Damon, but in other relationships, in other lives, we both had different names. Ah, but did we? Damon was a very unusual name in 1970. Did I remember it from another lifetime? What fun to guess and play with that! One day I will, when I deem it important, ask that question and bask in the answer.

Thank you for all you teach me. I loved hearing from Damon, but I am still saddened that the physical body is gone. (4-14-09)

"It is I, Amadeus. This day I wish for you to enjoy God's work, to love to teach. To not let jealousies interfere with your work. You, Sweet One, will rid yourself of self-destruction and rise out of the ashes whole and pure. Let this be the final day. Let us work toward a new beginning. No more pity, jealousy, or judgment. Let us work this day to practice what you preach. Go now in love and light, Amadeus."

So again, a gentle reminder that I am to purify my mind and thought patterns. I must begin anew and fresh from pain that will create self-pity, jealousy, and judgment. We do not always stay on our new path as well as we would like, but I brush myself off and move forward to become the very best I can be, as dictated from the Other Side by those who love me.

Last night, in my spiritual class, a fellow student, Katie, told a story about the two of us in a past lifetime that brought her to tears and sobbing. She had watched me be murdered for doing the work that I am doing now in this lifetime. Can you tell me about that lifetime and how we are playing it out in this lifetime? (4-19-09)

"Yes, this is Isaiah. Katie's Guide and I have been together many times when you and Katie have been on the Earth plane together. You and she have existed in other incarnates. Your names are not always the same, but your soul essence has been. In medieval times you were sisters. Note how in this incarnation you are both brown-haired and brown-eyed. You are Earth mothers. You have learned patience, and she wishes to continue to learn patience from you. As sisters, you were friends, but not alike. Through your role at the castle during this past life, you learned patience. You expect discipline, and with that perseverance follows. During that lifetime, you stood in line, quietly waiting for an allotment of food as your sister, Katie, would rather have someone else stand in line or steal food for her. In this current incarnation, she must practice standing in line herself and do what everyone else does. Later she can play, write, or meditate. Go forward in love and light, Isaiah."

I hope that she is learning patience, for she must learn this specific task in order to bring calm to her being. I find it interesting that we came together for that brief time and that we had no need to stay intertwined in this lifetime. I haven't yet learned exactly why we came together, and maybe I never will. Perhaps it was just to have her recognize herself in our past life together, and I had nothing to learn from that. It was probably her lesson and not mine at all. It's interesting, though, that here we have another example of reincarnating together repeatedly. Is this perhaps why I was shown her existence at that time? Was it to further my conviction in my teaching about reincarnation?

During a class meditation, we asked why there was war. (4-30-09)

"It is I, Amadeus. We continue to work in search of greatness. Each man and woman who gives their life for the cause they are fighting for moves to a higher plane. This does not mean they do not return, but when they do they have achieved higher knowledge of spirit. They have died violently, but return more docile and more ready to take and rationalize things, causing wars to be more sophisticated with less loss of mankind. It may not seem his way as you count bodies, but it is a fact. We are trying to help them to negotiate away from the nuclear path, which will destroy the Earth for centuries. This is a growth known by those who have crossed over and reincarnated. Go in peace, Amadeus."

By this revelation, you can see that our Guides and others see the devastation that is taking place in world politics and want to assist in saving us from our own destruction.

It is with that thought that I leave you to contemplate your place in all this. I know where mine is. It has been, and continues to be, a beautiful journey, and I can't wait to find out what's next as I write this in the fall of 2013. By the time you read these words, I know I'll have had many more memorable messages from Beyond, as they unfold with each meditation.

As I continued my journey in 2013, I was asked by Amadeus to work on healing the reactors in Fukushima, Japan, following the massive 9.0 earthquake and tsunami in March 2011. You will learn more about this later, as it needs its own special place in my story.

Chapter Twenty Seven

Learning to Communicate with Others in Spirit

It is I, Amadeus. Greetings, Dear Ones. YES, I welcome you to the knowing that will be found within this chapter of connection with the Other Side and all who have come and gone. Do not be frightened, as you have been to this juncture and will return again once more. Appreciate and love the story.

Go in Love and Light, Amadeus.

At this time, I am no longer involved with the mediumship class, but have become proficient, with practice, in knowing when my Guides and Others are sending me messages for students and seekers to hear. We bring forth, in Spirit Circle and at the Student Psychic Fair, Spirits who have crossed to the Other Side. These energies give us messages for the seekers, with that person's permission. One must never intrude in another's vibration without mutual agreement to do so.

My Guides have told me that practicing this modality of mediumship is the last piece of the puzzle that will make me whole and who I am meant to be in this lifetime. As stated earlier, this is a puzzle I was not aware of, but stepped into when the Universe directed me to help others heal the pain of loss by bringing messages from their loved ones forward. To lessen this pain by helping a grieving soul find solace in knowing their cherished one is at peace and always with them is my life's work.

My mediumship teacher, Debra, holds a Student Psychic Faire at the school where I volunteer and teach. It is there that we, as students in her class, give messages to anyone who is willing to let us practice on them. I have left her class on "Meeting and Working with your Guides," but continue to attend her Spirit Circle and the Student Psychic Fairs where I am able to hone my gift of mediumship. The first time I participated, I gave the sitter (the person receiving the messages) two sentences and was done. I heard a brief message, and with my insecurities and lack of trust in what I was doing, I quit asking for more information from my Guides who were working with me that night. Debra has worked hard with me to get me to give *all* the information I receive and to ask for more. She wants me to trust all that I am hearing and to share it, so that the sitter receives the entire message being sent. I've taken her advice, and today, with my Guides' and Angels' assistance, I am able to heal others' hearts. Oh, I could go on and on! I'm so grateful for this class, because without it, I would never have met my Guides or known their names and their reasons for being with me in this lifetime.

Justine speaks with me often, and I have come to know that she was my Gatekeeper through this class, when I was an active participant. (A Gatekeeper is one who decides what information is to be given to the sitter, and from which soul who is residing on the Other Side.) One night in class, we each asked, "Who is my Gatekeeper?" Then we meditated and remained quiet until we received the answer, which came as a name. We were all amazed at the information we received. When Justine came through for me, she explained that she's a Mothering Guide who helps when a heart is breaking, or when someone is in need of a gentle hug while I'm working with them to heal their heart.

To continue your education, dear readers, I will teach you as I have been taught by many in the psychic community. Your Guides are with you always, but they also allow Others their time with you, to write or to teach you lessons. I was told last night through my son, Damon, during a Spirit Circle, that I will channel many others before reaching my soul's true purpose. He did not tell me that purpose, as that is not for him to do.

A Spirit Circle is where many gather to bring in the White Light, Angels, Archangels, Guides and Others, and last (though certainly not least), those who have crossed into the Light and arrive to visit each of the participants. We can ask for a particular individual, but they do not always speak. The message you receive during this Circle is from whomever you are meant to receive it from. During the Circle, we give messages to each other and receive messages that we have heard from those on the Other Side. These messages are given by our own loved ones, with love to guide us more clearly on our path.

Amadeus has become known to me as my Master Guide. This is easy for me to believe, as he is the one who I write with most often and who has practical, loving advice for me and for all souls. Amadeus says that he and I have shared many lifetimes, so it is easy to understand why he appeared so early in my development and has steadfastly remained. I still visualize him as a wizened old man sitting in the Gazebo where I met him in 2007 and embraced his presence.

I have also learned through meditation that my Protector Guide is Chief Red Hawk. He shows himself with a stunning Native American headdress of magnificent hawk feathers! His upper body is not covered, except for a beaded bodice in turquoise and white. He wears a leather loin cloth and his feet are bare. His smile is dazzling and his stance exudes power. I am pleased that he always stands by me for my personal protection.

One evening in class, I was told that my Spiritual Advisor is Thor. Since the name was given to me by another student, and I did not receive it myself, I did not take it too seriously. Thor did say that amazing changes have come into my life, and that I was learning to trust and to listen. It was not until early 2013, when my teacher, Debra, instructed us to ask for the name of our Spiritual Advisor and I heard "I am Thor" pounding in my head, that I knew that what the other student had told me was true beyond any doubt.

Oh, how powerful was Thor! He bounded into the room with such mighty energy! As we each, in turn, gave a channeled message, I was the last to speak. When I did, Thor spoke loud and clear through me about healing Mother Earth and bringing this planet back into balance. Without a doubt, there is more we will hear from this Guide in the future.

I checked Wikipedia and learned that Thor was a hammer-wielding god conjured up in Norse mythology and associated with thunder, lightning, storms, oak trees, strength, and the protection of mankind. He shows himself to me, in my mind's eye, with billowing white robes and a lightning bolt in his hand. He is pure strength, although love pours from his eyes for Planet Earth.

It is with synchronicity that I met Thor again a few weeks after this class. I was teaching a class in Automatic Writing and Channeling one evening, and after a Guided Meditation by myself and my Guides, one of my students asked to speak with Amadeus. *"Good evening, Jon,"* Amadeus said to my student. *"I know you well, and you often have great questions for me. If there is ample time before the end of class, I will address your question."* Jon attends my lecture at the Holistic Faire at the end of each month, and he and Amadeus often chat and joke with each other.

This evening there was no joking. Amadeus asked Jon what his wishes were for the evening. It appears that after meditation during the automatic writing time, Jon had written with his Guides, asking them for his true purpose in life and what was it that he could do to assist in healing the damaged nuclear reactors in Fukushima, Japan. Amadeus boldly pronounced that Jon's purpose in this lifetime was to do just that!

***

As I continue my journey, I will undoubtedly meet all those who are assisting me, and perhaps someday, I will meet you, too. I invite you to pursue your spiritual growth by reading some of the books that you are pulled to when in the bookstore; they'll guide you along your path and inspire you further. You'll find, too, that the information presented here is substantiated by many revered authors, healers, mediums and teachers from many modalities. I ask you to take what you need and leave the rest.

Today, I continue to teach self-love and express thanks for the many blessings in my life. As Amadeus loves to say...

"Go in Love, Light and Laughter for Eternity. Amadeus."

Acknowledgements

I wish to thank, first and foremost, my husband, Kevin, for his support of this project. We both lost our son, Damon Andrew. Kevin grieves his way, and I grieve mine. Neither is right or wrong. Know that he never stood in my way as I pursued my spiritual path. He has been my rock, the foundation from which I move forward.

Many thanks to the rest of my immediate family: Michelle, the oldest; Kevin II, who is next; and Sean, the youngest. I include here all of their spouses and children. We continue to remember Damon and remind each other why he was special to us.

Morgan, thank you. Thank you for staying close and allowing us to be an integral part of your life. You are your daddy's gift to the family and its continuation through time.

Thank you to my sister, Janet, who wrote the Introduction for me. She has never forgotten a birthday of Damon's, and roses continue to arrive on my doorstep. We have shed many tears together as we remember the essence of who he was.

And a thank you to my sister, Marilyn, steadfast and true, and always there to remember him with me. The one who funded a gift to be given one day to Orange Coast College to support another aspiring chef – just as someone gifted Damon so many years ago. When my heart is ready, the gift will be presented.

And finally a shout-out of gratitude to all who made this book possible. Dr. Marjorie Miles, Dr. Heather Friedman-Rivera, Lillian Nader, Steve

Frances Pullin

Lesko and the others from "Writing with Your Dream Muse." This is a writing class led by Marjorie where we write without judgment and learn all about publishing our own books. Thanks to all of you for so many great tips! Thanks for all of the tips, all of you.

Thanks, too, to Joe Nunziata and Leonard Szymczak for their guidance and support of my writing and publishing through their classes and emails.

Please realize that this book would never have gotten off my computer and into your hands without the diligent assistance of my teacher and editor, Jean-Noel Bassior. I am in gratitude for her willingness to work with me over the past year and a half to bring my thoughts on paper to life! We put in many late nights, as she brought me to the best that is in me without once complaining. Thank you for all you have been to me and Amadeus.

Lisa Sakrison, thank you for proofreading the unedited, and then edited, versions of this book, along with my husband.

Many thanks to all my dear family and friends who have walked this journey with me. Too many to mention here, but know you are etched in my heart forevermore.

I want to remind my family, friends and teachers that the information written here is how I remember the story. I do not mean to tell it incorrectly, but the mind, being what it is, leads me to remember it my way.

I would also like to apologize to all of you who learned, like I did, that you never start a sentence with a preposition. I fought a strong battle over this with my awesome editor (a mainstream journalist specializing in celebrity interviews) – until she won! The sentences beginning with "and"

and "but" are part of my journey into the 21st century! Thanks, Jean-Noel, for persevering and walking me forward through my struggle!

I may be reached at angels-healing-hearts.com.

Many Blessings.

Endorsements

"In her book, It is I Amadeus, Channeled Messages From Sprit, Frances Pullin shares her powerful story about personal grief and how it led her to become a channel for important and loving messages from Spirit. I had the privilege of reading her very first draft, and I can't wait to read the book."

Marjorie Miles, DCH, MFT
Author "Healing Haikus"—a Poetic Prescription for Surviving Cancer

It is I, Amadeus is the fascinating tale of one woman's journey after the devastating loss of her son. She reveals how she began hearing messages from Spirit by channeling and how that led to helping others find healing. Author, Frances Pullin, tells her personal story with honesty, humor and love. It is a book of hope.

Heather Rivera, PhD,
Author of "Healing the Present from the Past" and *"Quiet Water"*

It is said that our souls make agreements prior to coming into the physical body in human form. When we are in the state of all-knowing and unconditional love, I imagine these decisions to be easier than they are to fulfill once we are in the body. It is also said that parents are "supposed" to die before their children. In this book, the mother remains here to be guided by her son from the unseen realms. When I read, It Is I, Amadeus, I was emotionally moved by the tremendous love that speaks from every page. The author, Frances Pullin, experiences a dramatic transformation from an everyday wife and mother to a gifted channel and medium. The price for these gifts is also part of the gift. The great loss of her precious son taught her without the shadow of a doubt that he still lives, speaks and touches her life.

It was the tragic loss of her son, Damon, that also led to this book of channeled messages from one called Amadeus, a very loving and powerful source of guidance not just for Frances, but for all who read her words. I recommend this book to anyone seeking spiritual awareness and inspiration to spark an awakening of the Soul and expansion of the mind.

Lillian Nader, M.Ed
Author of "Pandora," a musical comedy,
"Native Americans: A Proud Heritage," a workbook

Congratulations Frances on a heart-felt book about the healing power of spirituality! Undoubtedly a very difficult book to write, Frances poured out her soul for a greater cause.

Thank you, Frances, for candidly discussing some very painful memories in order to open the door for others to enter into the light so that they too can experience the healing benefits of Guided wisdom and unconditional love. It takes a pure spirit of love to be so devoted and so selfless.

Christina Gikas, C.Ht., Msc.D.

www.ingramcontent.com/pod-product-compliance
Lightning Source LLC
Chambersburg PA
CBHW032039290426
44110CB00012B/875